This is a comprehensive and up to date text book on Work Experience Education which is an important part of Indian school curriculum. This will be of much use to B.Ed. and E.T.E. pupil teachers, serving teachers and all other keenly interested in work experience and S.U.P.W.

General Books

LITERATURE

Iqbal Ramoowalia
The Death of a Passport 150.00
Mainak Dhar
Flash Point 195.00
Gurdial Singh
Earthy Tones 95.00
K. R. Wadhwaney
Scandel Controversies &
World Cup 2003 ....195.00
Dr. Giriraj Sah
Human Rights 195.00
A. K. Sharma
Clinton Levisky Scandal 60.00
Nostradamus and Prophecies
of the next Milleneum.........................195.00
Jaisankar Prasad
Kamayani 50.00
Brindawan Lal Verma
Toote Kante.......................................150.00
Aditi
My Endless Journey 50.00
Rabindranath Tagore
Boat Accident
(Translation of नौकाडूबी) 95.00
Inside Outside
(Translation of घरे बाइरे) 95.00

HISTORY AND BIOGRAPHIES

Lokesh Thani & Rajshekhar Mishra
Sensational Sachin 60.00
K.R. Wadhwaney
Scandals and Controversies
of World Cup 2003............................195.00
Virendar Kumar
Kargil : The Untold Story Rape of
the Mountain (With Pictures) 95.00
R.N. Sanyal
Freedom Struggle of India 95.00
Dr. B. R. Kishore
Chess for pleasure 60.00
Joginder Singh
Without Fear or Favour 195.00
Discovery of Independent India 195.00
B. K. Chaturvedi
Power to power 30.00
Chanakya Neeti 95.00
Kautilya's Arthashastra 95.00
Famous Tourist Centres of India 95.00

BIOGRAPHIES

Meena Agrawal
Indira Gandhi 95.00
Rajiv Gandhi 95.00
B. R. Kishore
Neelkanth (Lord Shiva)........................95.00
Gajanan 95.00
Hanuman 95.00
Goddess Durga 95.00
Lord Buddha 15.00
Lord Rama 15.00
Lord Krishna.......................................10.00
Asha Prasad
Swami Vivekanand 120.00
Mahesh Sharma
Ramkrishna Paramhans 95.00
Dr. A.P.J. Abdul Kalam 95.00
Atal Bihari Vajpayee 95.00
Lal Krishna Advani...............................95.00
Dr. Bhawan Singh Rana
Chhatrapati Shivaji 95.00
Bhagat Singh 95.00

FICTION

Abhimanyu Unnuth
Slices from a Life *(Memories of great writer of Mauritius)* **95.00**
R. N. Vyas
A New Vision of History 195.00
Swaran Chandan
The Volcano
(A Novel on Indian Partition) 195.00

Work Experience Education

Satya Pal Ruhela
Retired Professor of Education,
Head & Dean of Education,
Jamia Millia Islamia (Central University)
New Delhi-110025

DIAMOND BOOKS

ISBN : 81-288-1211-4

Published by : DIAMOND BOOKS (P) LTD.
X-30, Okhla Industrial Area, Phase - II
New Delhi - 110 020
: Phone : 011-41611861
: Fax : 011-41611866
E-mail : sales@diamondpublication.com
Website : www.diamondpublication.com

First Edition : 2006

Price : Rs. 95/-

Laser Typesetting: R. S. Prints Ph : 55136130

Printed by : Adarsh Printers,
Navin Shahdara, Delhi-110032

Work Experience Education
by : Prof. S.P. Ruhela Rs. 95/-

Contents

Introduction

"Education imparted through activities relieves the tyranny of purely academic and theoretical work it balances the intellectual and practical elements of experience and helps the child to be curious and satisfy his curiosity while doing and discovering things for himself."

—Dr. Zakir Husain

Work Experience has been given an important place in the school curriculum in India so that the gap between the students' knowledge and practical activity may be bridged. This develops the capacity to understand one's environment, abilitity to take part in the life activities, various values and smartness in children.

Gandhiji had given a prominent place to 'craft' in his scheme of '*Buniyadi Talim*' (Basic Education) in 1938. Basic Education survived till 1955 and thereafter, it was discarded. The *Education Commission* (1964-66) introduced the concept of '*Work Experience*' in place of the concept of 'Craft Education' in the Basic Education Scheme. This was introduced in Indian schools at all stages of school education. However, a new term SUPW (Socially Useful Productive Work) was introduced by the Central Government in the school curriculum to replace the concept of '*Work Experience*' at the recommendations of Ishwarbhai Patel Committee Report and Adisheshiah Committee Report in the later half of the 1970's. However, the concept of '*Work Experience*' is still more popular than the concept of SUPW. Most of the school teachers still think that 'Work Experience' is a more serious and useful concept than the SUPW and the real spirit of it is appreciated and followed by them while imparting instructions in SUPW subject in schools. Call SUPW or WE (Work Experience) now, the spirit and content is generally considered to be the same by the Teacher Educators of DIETs (District Institutes of Educational Training) and teachers of the Primary, Secondary and Senior Secondary Schools.

However, it is seen that most of the educationists, teachers and educational inspectors are not happy with the way SUPW or Work Experience is being taught in schools. As a matter of fact, most of the teacher educators are themselves not yet aware of the meaning, bases, contents, teaching strategies and related aspects of Work Experience. That is why they are not able to train the teachers under ETE (Elementary Teacher Education) and B.Ed. (Bachelor of Education) courses properly. The theoretical part of Work Experience is not being taught to the pupil by the teachers properly in many of the DIETs. There has been a scarcity of good books on the theory of Work Experience which the pupil-teachers can read and understand in order to learn why and how to teach Work Experience or SUPW to their students in schools.

This textbook, "*Work Experience Education*" has been written by me in order to meet this urgent need. I have carefully collected all relevant information from different sources and presented the same in a lucid, comprehensive and straight forward manner. Wherever necessary, a healthy criticism of the scheme and practices connected with this scheme of Work Experience has also been offered. An effort has been made to make the readers aware of the concept of 'Work Experience' and also the latest ideas, views and data relating to it.

Many teacher educators and pupil-teachers might like to study this in depth. For their guidance, I have included a comprehensive 'Bibliography' at the end of this book.

It is earnestly hoped that this textbook on Work Experience Education will be widely appreciated by the teachers of Work Experience, teacher educators and enlightened public, not only in India, but in the neighbouring countries also.

S.P. Ruhela
Retired Professor, Head
& Dean of Education Faculty,
Jamia Millia Islamia (Central University)
New Delhi-110025

126, Sector 37
Faridabad

1
Work and Its Importance

"All work, even cotton-spinning is noble, work alone is noble"

— Carlyle

Work is the most important and crucial thing in human life. The Oxford Dictionary has explained the concept or term of Work as under:

Work (noun) :
1. Expenditure of energy, striving, appreciation of effort to some purpose.
2. Tasks (to be) undertaken.
3. Things done, achievement, thing made book or piece of literacy or musical composition, literacy or other product.
4. Doing or experience of specified kind.
5. Employment, labour.

Work (verb) :
1. Engage or to be engaged in bodily or mental work, carry on operation, make efforts, be a craftsman.

It is clear from this that work is a kind of labour which is done on behalf of physical or mental effort, for some purpose.

The implication of work is that one leaves aside lethargy and engages himself or herself in some purposeful effort or activity. While doing any work, one has to concentrate his attention on a certain activity. He has to make full efforts, make use of his skills, physical and mental energy, control his emotions, keep them in balance and observe several values, virtues, ideals, norms and considerations.

A person has to do work according to the nature, kind, quality, importance or seriousness of the work or activity he is engaged in. He has to remain engaged in that activity for a considerable period of time. On the one hand he feels fatigue or tiredness by doing the work labouriously, on the other hand, he gets satisfaction and inherits various kinds of experiences which help in his mental, social, economic and intellectual development. No experience of any work, i.e. no work experience, goes to waste. Remaining engaged in work is life. In learning the art of living, work is an essential element.

Work can be of mental kind as well as of physical kind. In mental works, the mind has to make efforts. Often senses of the body have to make less efforts, as in these activities mainly the mind has to do most of the effort, e.g. reading a book, thinking of an idea, concepts or plan, understanding the implications of a concept or theory, writing a lecture, summary of any given written or spoken material, delivering a lecture, discussing certain points in a discussion etc. In most of the mental work or activities, the concerned person has to make less efforts or movements of hands and feet. That is why, the bodies of persons doing mental work mainly all the time are usually seen to be weak, and their senses are not found to be well-developed, well-trained, well-coordinated and their experiences are often found to be limited.

In physical work, all the organs, especially the sensory organs of the body have to involved. Therefore, they are developed. The person doing that work derives a great deal of satisfaction and experience. The more one works with a great deal of enthusiasm, labour and interest for a longer time, the more he is likely to achieve measure of success in that work. The importance of work has been described by various schools in their various significant questions. On the whole, they have emphasized that by doing work, a person gets a great deal of satisfaction. Not only this, he or she gets relief from worries, pain and pensiveness, and develops sociability, self-confidence, extroversion and skills, learns the art of living and thus his or her future is formed. Work is a great learning resource. It expands the mental and emotional horizons of the person doing the work.

When one is engaged in work, particularly physical work, and remains away from idle and evil thoughts, he goes on the right track of social and human values and thus, becomes a right kind of human being. Labourers and farmers doing hard physical labour lead healthy and happy lives inspite of their physical and economic deprivations. They lead a contented, peaceful and simple life. Work is not only a means of earning livelihood, but a valuable means to live a meaningful life.

Let us see and ponder over the following select quotation on work given by various scholars which reveal the importance of work in human life.

Some Valuable Quotations on Work

- "I believe in work, hard work and long heavy hours of work; rendered breakdown from over work, but from worry and dissipation."

  —Charles E. Hughes

- "Work well done today is the greatest possible half to better work tomorrow.

  —C.M.S.

- "Work keeps at bay three evils—boredom, vice and need."

  —Voltaire

- "The beauty of the work depends upon the way we meet it."

  —Anonymous

- "Work does more to dignify man or the individual than high official or public praise"

  —Ruskin

- "Work is not only a way to make a living, it is the way to make a living.'

  —Anonymous

- "Work is an investment and almost always pays."

  —Carleton

- "All time work is sacred. In all time work, were it but the true hard labour, there is something of divine-man"

  —Carlyle

- "All work, even spinning is noble, work alone is noble."

  —Carlyle

- "Work is not end in itself; through work, one must build up character and achieve all round development of his life."

  —Subhas Bose

It should be noted that the importance of work, especially physical work, has been realized by all parents in their families, all educationists in their schools, all religious and spiritual leaders in their monastries, nunneries and *ashrams*, all authorities in correction homes, jails, orphanages and welfare agencies. Even in higher education institutions, where a lot of emphasis is laid on theoretical or mental work, it is now being increasingly recognized that students should be involved in some sort of physical work as well, in order to ensure their balanced personality development.

Let us conclude by recalling the great words of Swami Vivekananda:

> "You must remember that all work is simply to bring out the power of the mind, which is already there to wake up the soul."

2
Work Experience: Definition & Objectives

"Work Experience has been defined as a participation in productive work in school, in the home, in the workshop, on a farm, in a factory or in any productive situation."

—H.P. Rajguru

For the last 40 years, the concept of 'Work Experience' has been a much talked about concept in Indian education. It is a desirable development but unfortunately it has been taken lightly, carelessly and in a confused manner. Few try to understand its theoretical implications.

Work Experience

In the first chapter, we have already mentioned that the dictionary meaning of 'Work' is making effort, doing some physical or mental activity involving labour, engaging oneself in some work, operation or activity.

How can a person get the experience, feel, knowledge of the work that he/she is doing? How can a person teach, guide, control, educate or socialize a young person, educate a student so that he/she gets experiences whether sour, bitter and pleasant? All these constitute the warp and woof of "*Work Experience*".

Althought the concept of Work Experience had originally developed in foreign countries, it was adopted in India for the first time by the 'Kothari Commission' or 'Education Commission' (1964-66) which was headed by Professor D.S. Kothari.

It was defined by the Education Commission in the

following words:

"Work experience involves participation in some form of productive work under conditions approximating to those found in real life situations..".

—*Report of the Education Commission, 1964-65, p. 201.*

It was mentioned in the Education Commission Report that since the Indian school education had become very academic and bookish, the concept of work experience would try to reform or correct it. In pages 8.72 to 8.78 and pages 201-203 of that report, many points relating to the meaning, importance and suggestions for implementing this concept were mentioned for the information and guidance of the teachers, teacher educators and all those interested in school education.

In his article, "Work Experience: A Critique of Education Commission Recommendations" published in a publication of the NCERT entitled '*Seminar on Primary and Work-Oriented Education*,' H.P. Rajguru defined Work Experience as under:

". . . (it) is participation in productive work in school, in the home, on a farm, in a factory or in any productive situation.'

The National Policy of Education (NCP) – 1986 defined Work Experience thus:

"Work Experience, viewed as a purposive and meaningful manual work, organized as an integral part of the learning process and resulting into either goods or services useful to the community, is considered as an essential component at all stages of education, to be provided through well-structured and well-graded programme."

—*In Service Teacher Education Package for Primary Teacher* (Vol. I), NCERT, March 1988, *p.* 167.

In that important document, the following points related to Work Experience were emphasized:

(1) The importance of work in the learning process.
(2) Something should be created or produced, or some service should be done through Work Experience.
(3) The importance of Work Experience should be accepted in the Indian school system.
(4) The nature of works or activities done in school should match the interests, capabilities and need of the learners i.e. students.

A well known expert on Work Experience, S.C. Choudhari of the N.C.E.R.T., had in his article, 'Work Experience and Vocationalization' published in the NCERT's '*Journal of Indian Education*' (May 1975), had made these important observations which ought to be understood and appreciated by all teachers and teacher educators:

"The concept of Work Experience developed by the NCERT in seminar, defines this activity as need-based, problem-solving, forward-looking, realistic, productive and manual. Accordingly, it includes work related to the basic needs of man namely, food, shelter, clothing, health and recreation. Later on, the areas of transport and communication were also added."

—*Journal on Indian Education,*
Vol. I, No. 1, May, 1975, P. 43.

In March 1998, the author of this book interviewed Prof. Vineeta Kaul, former Head of the Department of Pre-Primary & Primary Education, NCERT, and asked her about the latest position on the concept of 'Work Experience', according to her and her department in the NCERT. She informed him as under:

— The aims or objectives of Work Experience come very close to those of General Education.
— Its main emphasis is on desirable healthy living practices, environmental cleanliness and beautification of home, school and environment.

The NCERT publication on '*Minimum Levels Learning in Work Experience*' (especially its chapter No. 7) has underlined these points and school teachers should benefit from it.

Objectives of Work Experience

The objectives of Work Experience have been identified as under:

1. ***To make children forward-looking and modern:***

"Work Experience must be forward-looking in keeping with the character of the new social order."

— *Education Commission* (1964-66)

2. ***To make education purposeful:***

According to S.L. Gajwani, a former expert on 'Work Experience' in the NCERT, the main objective of introducing 'Work Experience' in the Indian school curriculum was to make education purposeful and adapt it as per the needs of the child, his/her family and community.

3. ***To develop character of the students***:

Proper values, attitudes and world-view should be developed by involving school children in work activities.

4. ***To bridge the gulf between manual work and mental work***:

Gandhiji had emphasized this point very forcefully in his valuable gift to the Indian nation in the form of '*Buniadi Talim*' (Basic Education) in 1938. Even before Gandhiji, ancient *Vedic Gurus* and Acharyas in India and Western thinkers like Tolstoy, Certyle, Bacon and many Christian Educators had emphasized this crucial point in their discussions and writings.

5. ***To make children appreciate the work done by labourers, farmers, and other manual workers in society***:

The children should not become elite-minded personalities, they should not develop highbrow attitude. They should learn to understand the importance of practical work, manual work and all roots of ordinary workers, labourers and the so-called proletariat, (as Karl Marx called them), in their society. They must understand what hardship, the so-called 'petty' or ordinary workers like carpenters, workers of the construction industry, cobblers, barbers, oilmen, road workers, painters, iron workers, gardeners etc. undergo and how they earn doing these hard and yet low paid manual activities. The 'Work Experience' subject learnt by the students in their schools is likely to make the students appreciate the work done by these workers and empathise with them. This will make them practical citizens who are well socialized.

6. ***To make children cooperative and integrated personalities***:

The students have most of the 'Work Experience' and SUPW (Socially Useful Productive Work) activities in school in small groups or batches. This develops the feeling of accommodation, adjustment, convention, integration, assimilation, which are socially integrative processes and crucially important for the making of a balanced social being, and a well developed citizen.

7. ***To make children appreciate manual work:***

The National Curriculum for Primary and Secondary Education prepared by the NCERT in 1985 had treated the concept of 'Work Experience' and the 'SUPW' as almost the same or identical. It clearly mentioned that the Work Experience and SUPW would go a long way in making children appreciate the importance of doing manual work, and inculcate social values like cooperation, self-dependence, taking initiative, industry or presence of sense and responsibility which will help them to become full-fledged personalities.

8. ***To promote social and productive efficiency in children***:

The Work Experience and SUPW activities would clearly promote social efficiency to a great degree and also promote productive efficiency to some degree.

The Directorate of School Education, Delhi State, in April 1991, laid down the following two broad fields or areas of the objectives or Work Experience:

i. ***Cognitive field***: Objectives relating to knowledge, understanding about work, work experience.
ii. ***Skill Field***: Objectives relating to skills which should and would be developed in children through such practical activities.

Objective of Providing Work Experience

According to the NCERT, the objectives of providing Work Experience are:

- To acquaint children with the world of work and occupation and to derive in them, a sense of respect for manual workers.
- To develop in children an awareness of social problems and include in them a positive attitude towards community sense.
- To develop in them a desire to be useful workers of the society and to contribute their best to the common good.
- To inculcate in them a positive attitude towards team work and socially desirable values like self-reliance, dignity of labour, tolerance, cooperation, sympathy and helpfulness.
- To help them in understanding the principles involved in various forms of work.

• To motivate children to participate increasingly in productive work, as they go from one stage of education to another, thereby enabling them to inculcate as they learn.

• To provide opportunities for creative self-expression and for the development of problem solving abilities.

The NCERT publication *Work Experience In School Education* (1987) had broadly emphasized that the objectives or aims of teaching Work Experience in Indian schools are of three kinds:

I. Objectives related to knowledge and understanding
II. Objectives related to competence, capability and capacity to do practical activites
III. Objectives related to behaviour and values

It should be clearly noted by the teachers, teacher educators as well as the public and the students that Work Experience includes both kind of activities: (a) manual work or work done by hand, as well as (b) social services which aim at providing help or relief to the society in one way or the other, and (c) activities which make the students aware of the environment, ecology or nature and its processes and usual and unusual changes.

Efforts have been made by the NCERT, the School Education Departments or Boards of different Indian States to develop a stage-wise aims and contents of the subject of 'Work Experience' in school education in :

(a) Primary Class (I-V Stage)
(b) Upper Primary Class (VI – VIII) Stage
(c) Secondary (IX – X Stage)

The stage-wise curriculum should be seen and appreciated by the teachers, teacher educators, teacher trainees and school students.

Time allotted to Work Experience & Art Curricular activities are:

Classes I – II	25 per cent of daily school time
Classes III – V	20 per cent of daily school time
Classes VI – X	10.5 per cent of daily school time.

Some Landmarks in Work Experience

- Earn while you learn scheme (Madhya Pradesh)
- Camp Life of students of classes IX – X (five days group for Each Class) (Rajasthan)
- Mandal Vocational Education Centres (Andhra Pradesh)

(28 Mandal Vocational Education Centres)

Details of these three landmarks of Work Experience Education can be seen from A.K. Sacheti's article on 'Work Experience', published in the *Encyclopedia of Indian Education*, NCERT, 2004

Statement of the N.P.E. (National Policy in Education), 1986, on Work Experience

The National Policy on Education (1986) reiterated the concept of Socially Useful Productive Work and renamed it as Work Experience. In this context, it laid down the following as a policy statement:

Work Experience, viewed as purposive and meaningful manual work, organized as an integral part of the learning process and resulting in either goods or services useful to the community, is considered an essential component at all stages of education, to be provided through well-structured and graded programmes. It would comprise activities in accordance with the interests, abilities and needs of students, the level of skills and knowledge to be upgraded with the stages of education. This experience would be helpful to one's entry into the workforce. Pre-vocational programmes provided at the Lower Secondary Stage will also facilitate in the choice of the vocational courses at the Higher Secondary Stage.

The above statement provides:

— a definition, which underscores the significance of work in the learning process, the need for a product or service emerging out of the work performed, the universality of work in the school system and beyond, and the need for well-structured and well-graded programmes.

— a clue to the nature of work activities so as to conform to the interests, abilities and needs of the learner.

— a case for increasing the skill level to match the stage of education.

— the purpose of such will help in: (I) smoother transition to the world of work, and (ii) predisposition to the selection of a particular vocation for a majority of students.

One of the distinctive features of the Work Experience Programme as visualized in the National Policy, is the provision of pre-vocational programmes at the high school stage.

3
SUPW: The Concept and Its Implications

"SUPW may be described as purposive and meaningful manual work, resulting in either goods or services which are useful to the community."

—Report of the Review Committee

The concept of SUPW in Education

The concept of 'Socially Useful Productive Work' in education is one of the most recent concepts in Indian education. It had been developed out of Mahatma Gandhi's educational ideas which laid stress on work-centered education having practical utility to society. In the scheme of Basic Education, which was mainly meant for the social regeneration of the rural society, Gandhiji laid a great deal of emphasis on organizing various activities in Basic School to provide socially useful and productive experiences to children. This was aimed at bringing children closer to the real understanding of social-economic, cultural and political needs, expectations and aspirations of their society.

Basic School provided a valuable experience to children for a number of years, but unfortunately due to several reasons, Basic Education lost its popularity during the decade of 1961-70. Consequently, the emphasis laid by Gandhiji on Socially Useful Productive Work was also soon forgotten by educational planners and administrators.

The Kothari Commission (1964-66), proposed the concept of 'Work Experience' to be implemented in Indian school. It sought to provide practical experience in activities and in processes of modern life. In 1975, the National Council of

Educational Research & Training, New Delhi, published the curriculum for the Ten Year framework and also a number of textbooks according to that curriculum. This evoked criticism from the public. Therefore, the Union Education Minister appointed in June 1977 a Review Committee under the chairmanship of Ishwar Bhai Patel, the then Vice-Chancellor of Gujarat University, to review the curriculum for the Ten year school.

This Review Committee re-emphasized the need for providing practical, useful, productive, socially relevant and educative activities in schools like the ones Mahatma Gandhi had earlier suggested in his scheme of Basic education. It recommended that 'Socially Useful Productive Work' (SUPW) must be the central content and the academic subjects of the school should be related to it as far as possible.

> *"Socially Useful Productive Work may be described as purposive and meaningful manual work resulting in either goods or services which are useful to the community."*
>
> — *Report of the Review Committee on the Curriculum for the Ten Year School, 1977.*

You may like to know the implications of the three adjectives, namely, 'Socially', Useful' and 'Productive' work.

The report of the Review Committee, headed by Ishwar Bhai Patel had given explanations of the terms. Further these were clarified in a National Workshop on 'Socially Useful Productive Work: Concept and Implementation' organized by the Faculty of Education, Gujarat Vidhyapith, Ahmedabad, from October 15 - 18 in 1978.

The meaning of '*socially*' in this concept is that a child who has attained a minimum level of education, should be able to function efficiently in his or her community, both in respect of social skills and work skills and also in terms of adjustment to the immediate group. The emphasis is implied on the needs and interests of the growing child, because his or her vital interest basically includes the need for effective participation and proper functioning in society.

The meaning of '*useful*' is that the work should lead to something that is useful to the child (as a medium for all round growth) and also to the general group, community or society in terms of returns.

By '*productive*' it is meant that the product or service (whether concrete or abstract) should be a useful addition to existing resources or practices of the community. The productivity may be measured in terms of tangible or intangible outcomes. It may be in terms of money earned, unearned or saved by the school, or in terms of development of good values and attitudes .

Socially Useful Productive Work:

Socially : The work activity should be socially relevant and meaningful.

Useful : The activities and products arising thereof, should be functional to the needs of the child and the society.

Productive : The activity should result in products or services which are socially consumable.

What are the Foundations of SUPW?

The concept of SUPW is based on sound foundations of education. Let us briefly consider its philosophical, sociological, economic, physiological and psychological foundations.

(A) Philosophical Foundations

The Ishwar Bhai Committee had stated that the concept of Socially Useful Productive Work should be developed in the light of the Gandhian philosophy of Basic education. You know that Mahatma Gandhi's social philosophy was that of the development of the 'Sarvodaya Samaj' based on ideals of high moral, social, cultural and economic values, humanism, socialism, cooperation, equality, freedom from exploitation of the individual and decentralization. The individual must be self-sufficient, moral, efficient and guided by the high values of freedom, initiative, cooperation, social service, self-discipline, truth and patriotism.

Our Constitution seeks to make our country a democratic socialist secular nation based on the philosophical values and notions for which Gandhi stood. By providing opportunities to children to engage themselves continuously in a variety of socially useful productive work, they are bound to grow up as enlightened citizens having the right kind of democratic philosophy.

(B) Sociological Foundations

The traditional education emphasizing the 3 R's has been responsible for a divide between those who got educated and those who do not work manually. This barrier has to be removed by SUPW. The children have to be made sensitive to the needs, demands, aspirations and problems of the Indian society. The cultural traditions of our society are also to be properly understood and followed. The SUPW activities seek to make our children committed to the socially desired values, attitudes and beliefs worthy of democratic secular citizens. They are so planned as to make them aware of what our culture and society have to offer them, what their potentialities for growth are, and how and to what extent growth, development, change, reform and modernization are to be achieved. The Ishwar Bhai Committee Report had rightly pointed out that "The component of social service in the curriculum is allied to SUPW. For example, when children participate in an environmental cleanliness programme by way of social service, they can simultaneously prepare pits for composite manure. Similarly, if children conduct surveys of population, habitations or cattle, they can use this information for planning programmes related to childcare and sanitation. During the harvesting season, when the entire village is under pressure of intensive work, the schools, instead of remaining in isolation, can render valuable help" (1977).

(C) Economic Foundations

The basic idea of SUPW is to provide activity-based education, which may serve as an important social investment in the life of the students as well as of the community. By learning to do several activities of daily life with his own hands and with the resources locally available, the child becomes self-sufficient, thrifty, economically productive and useful to himself, his family and his community. While doing various kinds of manual activities, he may develop a fair amount of expertise in one or more of them, and adopt it as his life occupation as well, if necessary. In order to ensure rural development, it is necessary to attract, train and re-train as many people in rural arts and crafts as possible. The rural-urban migration also has to be checked. The SUPW activities thus, show as a ray of hope in regeneration of the rural score also.

(D) Physiological Foundations

For a healthy development of body, physical exercise is very necessary. By involving themselves in manual work related to making of things and in social services children will undergo, naturally and indirectly, the much needed bodily exercise and sense-training. Not only will their muscles grow stronger, their circulatory and digestive systems will also function well as a result of the physical labour done by them daily in schools under the SUPW programme.

(E) Psychological Foundations

Children love activity. A child when left alone, reveals interest in conversation, in construction, in artistic expressions, in collecting various attractive things and in games. He is eager to interact with his immediate environment. Learning by doing interests him very much. The process of socialization is of supreme importance to him. His love for play, for acquiring integrated knowledge, for activity, for group-involvement and his need for sense-training and multi-faceted growth—physical, social, moral, intellectual, aesthetic, have been recognized by all great educationists. By organizing SUPW activities, a child's personality and learning can be enriched and his mastery on the environment and the development of his values, attitudes, aspirations etc. can also be promoted. The SUPW activities can provide good media for the sublimation of the child's instincts.

Foundations of SUPW

***Philosophical*:** Based on the social philosophy of humanism, equality, secularism, decentralization and self-discipline.

***Sociological*:** Emphasis on removing the barrier between work and mental work, development of socially relevant values and attitudes, and making the children sensitive to the needs, aspirations and problems of the society.

Economic : Emphasis on self-sufficiency, thrift, economic productivity, and checking rural-urban migration.

Physiological: Need to do ample physical exercise for healthy body and healthy mind, proper development of senses.

Psychological: Sublimation of instincts, proper growth of child, socialization and need to control on the immediate environment. Emphasis on 'Learning by doing' and 'Group activity'.

II

What are the Various Kinds of Activities Covered Under the Concept of Work Experience?

The objectives of providing Socially Useful Productive Work Experience are as under:

(i) To acquaint the children with the world of work and the productive occupations going on in the community and to develop in them a sense of respect for manual workers.

(ii) To develop in the children, an awareness of social problems and inculcate in them, positive attitudes towards community service.

(iii) To develop in them a desire to be useful members of the society and to contribute their best to the common good.

(iv) To inculcate in them, a positive attitude of teamwork and socially desirable values, like self-reliance, dignity of labour, tolerance, cooperation, sympathy and helpfulness.

(v) To help them in understanding the principles involved in the various forms of work.

(vi) To lead the children to participate increasingly in productive work, as they go from one stage of education to another, thereby, enabling them to earn while they learn.

(vii) To provide opportunities for creative self-expression and for the development of problem-solving abilities.

The contents of Socially Useful Productive Work should

be basic to the needs of the child, the school and the community. Therefore, it should be very flexible in nature. The total programme of SUPW will have two components, viz. a core programme comprising simple activities belonging to the six need areas, viz. food, shelter, health, recreation, community work and social service. These activities will not require much investment. The other activity will be an elective component concerned with work practice, comprising production of goods and services related to the needs and facilities available.

From the point of view of the learning and skill development process, experience in every productive work or service has to be provided in three phases, viz.: (i) exploration of the world of work with the help of observation, discussion and very simple manipulation, (ii) experimentation with materials, tools and techniques, and (iii) work practice in the form of work projects or crafts, trades and services. This aspect should be reflected in the planning of the contents.

While selecting the activities, the following criteria ought to be kept in view:

1. To be educative, the activities should
   - (i) Be according to the development level of the children.
   - (ii) Cater to the developmental needs of the children.
   - (iii) Help to develop the total personality of the children.
   - (iv) Help in the process of their self-realization.
   - (v) Be planned enterprises involving problem-solving skill and creative thinking.
   - (vi) Help in value formation.
   - (vii) Help children acquire relevant knowledge, skills, etc. and
   - (viii) Help children to grow as efficient workers.
2. To be productive, the activities should result in
   - (i) Either products which are (a) directly consumable by the children and the community, particularly, the school community, and if need be (b) saleable; or
   - (ii) Services having social and economic values.
3. To be socially useful, the work should be relevant to meet the needs of the community and the individual child.

In addition to the above mentioned fundamental criteria,

the following criteria should also be considered:

(i) Necessary tools, materials, techniques, facilities are readily available.

(ii) Adequate resources and persons should be available.

(iii) It should be feasible enough to carry out the activity to useful completion.

The programme is not limited to the development of neuro-motor skills only. It also involves cognitive learning and it ensures significant effective growth.

Productive manual work situations relating to production of goods and services will have to be drawn from the areas of health and hygiene, food shelter, clothing, culture and recreation and community work and social service. These work situations occur at home, in school and in the community. Such programmes will have two components—a common core programme and work practice.

How Should SUPW be Implemented in School?

Due care should be taken in giving practical shape to the concept of SUPW. No headmaster, teacher or educational administrator should blindly accept any list of SUPW activities. It is desirable that the social plans suit activities with the thorough consultation of all the teachers, student leaders and monitors. This plan should be discussed with various individuals in the community, viz. *panchayats*, political and social workers of the area, officers of the various government and autonomous organizations and workers, artisans etc. The teachers have to be constantly alert and eager to make the best possible use of whatever opportunities come to them for making SUPW activities useful, not only to the students, but also to the members of the community as a whole.

The teachers should realize and keep three things in mind while planning and executing such work activities. Firstly, they should try to plan within the financial resources of the school and secondly, with the activity staff. No additional teachers will be made available to the school. Thirdly, SUPW has to be a need-based programme with emphasis laid on local specifics. There ought to be some difference in the activities for rural schools and urban schools, for boys and girls, and for different classes of the school. The local environment must be properly assessed by the teachers so that they can decide as to which activities are "Must activities" "Should activities", or "Can-could activities".

Strategy for Implementation of SUPW in School

A proper strategy for the implementation of SUPW in school should consist of the following logical and useful steps:

1. ***Survey of the existing resources in the school***: This should be done by the teachers with the help of students and clerical staff.

2. ***Survey of the community***: This should be done by the teachers and students in order to collect such information as under:

(a) Different work situations available in the community.

(b) A likely number of students who can be attached to different work situations in the community.

(c) Community leaders.

(d) Need of the community for non-formal education.

(e) Number of units wherein students can participate in production.

(f) Members of the community who will be willing to render their cooperation, and the nature of their likely cooperation.

(g) Natural resources freely available.

3. ***Staff meeting***: To discuss and decide about the following:

(a) Which of the programmes can be started in the school without difficulty?

(b) What preparations are necessary for them?

(c) What sort of orientation should be provided to the students?

(d) What should be done to seek public cooperation?

(e) How will the duties be assigned to individual teachers?

(f) How will SUPW activities be assessed regularly?

4. ***Maintaining brief records of each student's participation and progress in SUPW.***

5. ***Assessment of the SUPW done by the students:***

It may be desirable to keep in mind the following considerations in the formulation of SUPW programmes:

(1) Age level of the students.
(2) Class level of the students.
(3) Size and type of school.
(4) Sex of the students.
(5) Immediate environment of the school.

The Ishwar Bhai Committee had suggested that coordinated efforts should be made for the implementation of the programme. High level committees should be constituted at all levels of the Central and State Governments. These committees should meet regularly to plan, implement and review the SUPW and to suggest improvements from time to time.

The implementation of SUPW in schools should be done intelligently and realistically. Due cooperation of all teachers, students village leaders and officials should be enlisted in the planning and administration of SUPW programmes in schools.

How Should SUPW be Evaluated in Schools?

The NCERT publication *Socially Useful Productive Work* Curriculum: Developing and Implementing the Programme (1979) made the following four broad suggestions in regard to the evaluation of SUPW programmes in schools:

1. When the programmc has run for one or two years, it may be evaluated with the help of a local team, with a view to identify the bottlenecks and improving the curriculum.

2. On the basis of the evaluation of the programmes, a small working group may be appointed by each school to analyze the outcomes of the evaluation of the programme and suggest action points to remove the bottlenecks for improving teaching-learning.

3. Extension work plays an important role in enriching the teaching-learning.

4. The programme of Socially Useful Productive Work is such, that it should assimilate new developments that are taking place in the production of goods and services, particularly, in the field of agriculture. Therefore, some liaison work has to be arranged between the Education Departments and the extension wings of the various departments, concerned with production and services.

Suggestions for the proper evaluation of SUPW activities in schools are as under:

1. The evaluation should be done at regular intervals throughout in the schools.

2. The evaluation should not be in the form of a paper on an academic subject. It should be comprehensive and practical in nature.

3. These ten areas should be evaluated: (I) Health and Hygiene; (ii) Food; (iii) Shelter; (iv) Clothing; (v) Culture and Recreation; (vi) Community Work and Allied Services; (vii) Proficiencies in a core programme for bringing about attitudinal changes; (viii) Work practices for giving vocational bias to programme; (ix) Efforts to bring the school and community closer to each other; and (x) Learning through work.

4. Teachers should develop some objectives and tools for evaluating the following aspects of SUPW:

(a) Time devoted by a student to each kind of activity.

(b) Whether done individually or collectively.

(c) Role of the student-trainer, evaluator, or participant.

(d) Student's involvement in SUPW on the following criteria:

Initiative, resourcefulness, regularity, punctuality, interest, quantity, and quality of output, cooperation, aesthetic tools, charts preparation, and maintenance of records, etc.

5. As far as possible, the evaluation should be done by that very teacher who conducts SUPW in that class. This evaluation should be done on one's own potential, daily or weekly.

6. A three-point scale (high degree, ordinary degree, low degree), or a five-point scale (excellent, good, satisfactory, poor, very poor) may be used in order to evaluate most of the above points.

7. In lower classes, (I-V), oral tests may also be conducted along with practical work. In higher classes (VI-XII), written papers may also be given.

8. Efforts should be made to see that the students enjoy being evaluated in SUPW rather than resenting it.

Select Refrerence for Further Study

1. *Concept of Basic Education.* New Delhi, Ministry of Education, Government of India, 1957.
2. *Concept of Work Experience.* New Delhi, NCERT, 1970.
3. *Examination Reform Programme of the NCERT.* New Delhi, NCERT, (Mimeographed, Year of publication not mentioned), pp.19-20.
4. Gandhi, M.K., *Basic Education.* Ahmedabad, Navjivan Publishing House, 1951.
5. *Report of the National Review Committee on Higher Secondary Education, with Special Reference to Vocationalization.* New Delhi, Ministry of Education & Social Welfare, Government of India, 1978.
6. *Report of the National Workshop on Socially Useful Productive Work* (Oct. 15-18, 1978). Ahmadabad, Gujarat, Vidyapith, Faculty of Education, 1970.
7. *Report of the Review Committee on the Curriculum for the Ten-Year School.* New Delhi, Ministry of Education & Social Welfare, Govt. of India, 1977, PP. 10-15; 127-128.
8. *Report of the Secondary Education Commission.* New Delhi, Ministry of Education, Govt. of India, 1953.
9. Ruhela S.P. & Vyas, K.C. *Sociological Foundations of Education in Contemporary India.* Delhi. Dhanpat Rai & Sons, 1970.
10. *Sample Curriculum Units in Socially Useful Productive Work.* New Delhi, NCERT, 1978.
11. *Socially Useful Productive Work Curriculum:* Developing and Implementing the programme. New Delhi, NCERT, 1979.

4
Work Experience: Historical Foundation

"I feel convinced that the salvation of the country will be far distant if we do not learn to honour the workman's tools, at least in a similar manner as the scholar's pen or the warrior's sword."

—Sir Sultan Ahmad
Convocation address at the
Aligarh Muslim University in 1926

The concept of 'Work Experience' was introduced in the Indian School Education System for the first time as recommended by the 'Kothari Commission' or 'Education Commission' (1964-66). But we should not forget that this concept has a long and rich historical background:

1. In the Stone Age, about 20,000 years ago, human beings lived in groups, made stone tools, hunted animals and birds and led a nomadic life. As hunters and food-gatherers, they trained their children in day-to-day practical life activities and thus their children gained work-experience by doing such activities.

2. In the agricultural stage of human civilization about 8-10 thousand years ago, human beings started doing agriculture in countries like Egypt, India, Mesopotamia, China, etc.

3. About 8-10,000 years ago, many pyramids and temples were built in Egypt. Several books on the history of Egypt, like Trigyer's '*Ancient Egypt: A social History*' (1983) and Elizabeth Hatch's '*Initiation*', inform us that there existed schools for the training of male and female priests in the ancient Egyptian temples. In those days, many kinds of work activities were done such as like cleaning, decoration,

gardening, ploughing, celebration of festivals and worshippings etc. which gave rich practical work experience to the young male priests and nuns.

4. In Pre-Vedic, Vedic and Post-Vedic civilisation (about 6000 – 2000 B.C.), students in the *Gurukuls* and *Ashrams* used to receive work experience in many kinds of practical work, manual work as well as social service work. They learnt many kinds of *Kalas* (arts) and crafts in those institutions like cutting wood and bringing it to their *ashram*, gardening and farming, woodwork, cleanliness, washing utensils. fineries, garments, chariots, huts, cooking food etc. A.S. Altekar's famous book '*Education in Ancient India*' and the *Purans* and *Mahabharta* inform us about these activities which provided matchless work experience to the students in those times.

5. In the ancient Greek civilization (3500 B.C.), and Roman civilization (about 2700 B.C.), various kinds of work/ activities like tool-making, house-building, sculpting, making of decoration pieces, war tools etc. were taught to students which gave a unique work experience to them.

6. The history of the rise and spread of the great religions of the world like Buddhism, Christianity and Islam reveal that every kind of work or activity like sculpting, house building, temple construction, making of statues, printing, decoration, arts etc., were done in their religious places and educational institutions.

7. In Europe, during 1492-1648, the Era of Reformation arose in which various arts and crafts flourished to great heights.

8. In India during the British colonical rule, many Indian arts and crafts were destroyed and were not allowed to grow by the foreign rulers who also destroyed the ancient literature and cultural heritage of India. They enforced book education and introduced the English system of education. The Indian culture, traditional Indian economy, and traditional arts and crafts were discouraged by them and were allowed to decay and die out.

9. Pioneering freedom fighters of India – Lokmanya Bal Gangadhar Tilak and Mahatma Gandhi worked for liberation and socio-economic and cultural awakening of the Indian society. Gandhiji strongly emphasized that in his scheme of Basic Education, craft activities, and socio-cultural activities

and physical nature activities education should be provided to children through correlation technique or 'correlated teaching' strategies. Several freedom fighters supporters and companions of Gandhiji like C. Ramchandran, Dr. Zakir Husain, Marjorie Sykes, Aryanyakam, Vinoba Bhave, etc. adopted and promoted this. Basic Education flourished between 1938 and 1966 but after that it was discarded.

10. In 1966, the *Education Commission* (1964-66) headed by the eminent Indian Professor, Daulat Singh Kothari, recommended that instead of education of crafts which was an integral part of Basic Education, the new concept of Work Experience should be adopted at all stages of the Indian School System. It is said that this concept was very popular in the earstwhile USSR and there was a Russian educator among the members of the Education Commission (1964-66) whose suggestions were duly appreciated and accepted by all the members of the commission. Thus Work Experience was introduced as a new subject in the Indian school curriculum at the primary and secondary levels.

11. In 1977, the Ishwar Bhai Committee was appointed by the Government of India. It mentioned that the concept of 'Work Experience' could not be properly understood by the school teachers in the country, and therefore, it could not be properly implemented in the school. It could not be made socially useful to the Indian society. Therefore, the Ishwar Bhai Committee recommended that in its place a wider, more comprehensive, all inclusive and useful concept of SUPW (Society Useful Productive Work) should be brought in the school curriculum. This recommendation was accepted by National Educational Conference held in New Delhi in 1977. It was decided that the daily time of a school should be divided as under:

- 50 per cent time for productive and creative work activities
- 50 per cent time for doing practical work activities

This meant that the earlier concept of Work Experience was elaborated, modified and modernized to make it socially relevant and functional to the needs of the Indian schools in contemporary, socio-cultural and economic contexts.

The Ishwar Bhai Committee defined SUPW as under:

"SUPW is viewed as purposive, and meaningful, manual work resulting in either goods or services which is useful to

the community."

It shows that Gandhi's idea of society relevant work activities was again revived and introduced in the school system under the SUPW subject.

In 1979, the C.B.S.E. (Central Board of Secondary Education), New Delhi, brought out a booklet, 'Society Useful Productive Work: Guidelines for Teachers' in which this concept was explained thus:

"From the conceptual point of view, SUPW is an extension of Work Experience, the scope of which has been extended to include 'services' in addition to goods. In Work Experience, it has been decided to give a forward look to basic crafts and provide the experience under a real production situation. In actual practice, it was felt that the Work Experience activities were mostly confined to the commercial activities concerned with acquisition of skills, production of goods and maintenance work within the four walls of the classroom and they were carried out rather mechanically. Therefore, while on the one hand, the scope of these activities was limited, on the other hand, they lacked social usefulness; instead they prepared the individual for his own self. More so, experience under real production situation was hardly made available.

Now in order to re-orient the on going programme of experience, it is necessary to:

(i) Enrich the programme by including activities that are relevant to the needs of the community. The activities may belong to the six areas mentioned : (1. Health and Hygiene, 2. Food, 3. Shelter, 4. Clothing, 5. Recreation and Cultural Activities, 6. Community Work and Social Service).

(ii) Adopt problem-solving approach and ensure student involvement in planning and execution.

(iii) Identify the relative knowledge and also develop work related projects resulting in the well-being of the community.

On 27th August 1977, the eminent Gandhian thinker, Dr. Sriman Narayan, delivered a lecture on 'New Education Pattern' in the NCERT. In his lecture he severely criticized the concept of Work Experience, having gone through the syllabus prepared by the NCERT.

The NCERT states that Work Experience at the primary stage should be 25 per cent of the total time. It is just 'Work Experience' and no correlation anywhere. As you go higher, it becomes less and less.' Gandhiji had said: "Self-sufficiency cannot be achieved at the primary level; it begins at the middle stage, higher school stage and at the college stage." But it is just the reverse now, i.e. high school having only two to four periods in a week. You are required only to certify that the student has done some kind of work experience – say two, three or four periods in a week. This is really unfair. We start with a good programme and swear that we are following Basic Education, as conceived by Gandhiji. NCERT also says that Work Experience which we have substituted for Basic Education, is the same as productive work in Basic Education. But when we implement these schemes, it becomes something else. It is to this which I object very seriously...".

—*'New Educational Pattern of 10+2+3' : NIE Lecture* by Dr. Shriman Narayan on 25 Aug. 1977.

In the various publications of the NCERT, somewhat varying interpretations of Work Experience and its *avatar* (incarnation) and SUPW were mentioned during 1979-1988, which fact is evident from the following excerpts of these publications:

• (3.41) The programme of SUPW is different from crafts. Crafts aim at developing manipulative skills only, whereas the former aims at promoting the harmonious development of his body, mind, heart and spirit.

• (3.42) The programme of Work Experience lacked the component of social usefulness and in practice, was not even casually correlated to other subjects. The remunerative aspect of this programme was given high priority at the cost of creative thinking, scientific planning and intelligent performance by going into the 'why' and 'where'.

• (3.43) Originating from the Gandhian concept of education, SUPW is a tool for inculcating Gandhian values, viz. truth, non-violence, self-reliance, dignity of labour, cooperation classless society, etc.

—*SUPW Curriculum* (NCERT, 1978)

• "Work Experience is a conscious effort to fill the gap between wanted and intellectual work, thus, giving a meaning and purpose to the learning process. The principal aim of Work Experience is to prepare children for life, equipping them with proper attitudes, knowledge and skills in respect of work."

—*Guidelines and Syllabi for Upper Primary Stage, Class VI-VIII*, NCERT (1988)

• "Work Experience or Socially Useful Productive Work should inculcate in the learners a respect for manual work.

—*National Committee for Primary and Secondary Education*, NCERT, Dec. 1985.

The above shows that till 1985 the NCERT treated Work Experience and SUPW as identical or one and the same concepts. Then why does the term, 'Work Experience' continue to be popular in its publications? This has created some confusion.

In the B.Ed Course of various universities like Kurukhastra University, M.D. University, Rohtak, etc., there is no proper programme on 'Work Experience' till now.

"The programme of Work Experience or Socially Useful Productive Work, in which Gandhiji's Basic Education laid stress, has not been implemented in most of the underlying concepts, which is logically unacceptable from the point of view of social relevance, work ethics as well as internalization of knowledge."

Challenge of Education: A Policy Perspective, Govt. of India, Aug. 1985, P. 36

The famous Gandhian thinker and educator, Acharya Vinoba Bhave, had stressed on the need for providing socially useful Work Experience to children in schools. In his remarkable book of ideas, *Shikshan Vichar*' (1955), he mentioned the following interesting points:

— "We get knowledge from activity (work) and with knowledge, the activity is accomplished, and with the meeting of both *gyan* (knowledge) and *carma*, mind develops."

— "Every activity or work done in school should become a medium of knowledge. For this, schools will have to be decorated and well-polished."

— "The main purpose of learning craft activity or practicals within schools is to develop social consiousness.

It may be of much interest to the readers of this book to know that a great leader, Subhas Chandra Bose had given his views that children must be taught though practical activities and with the help or various tools, musical instruments, and appliances. They should get training in making dolls, relief maps made of mud, drawing and painting, popular music etc. Their senses should be trained.

In pages 131-133 of the volume '*Subhas Chandra Bose – Correspondence*' his suggestion has been mentioned in detail which the readers of this book should see.

Dr. Zakir Husain, the great follower of Gandhiji and author of the Wardha Sharma of Education shared Gandhi's views on the importance of work in education of the children.

He recognized the importance of productive work in education and insisted on its quality. According to him :

"All work is not educative. It is educative only when it is preceded by mental effort. You have to first plan the work in your mind, then to think of the ways and means of doing it, then to perform it actually and finally, to assess the results and compare them with the guiding plan.

Only that work is generally educative which serves some higher value, higher than ones selfish ends, and to which we are devoted."

—S.P. Ruhela, 'Educational Contribution of Zakir Husain,' *University News*, Feb 9, 1987

Dr. Zakir Husain

5
Work Experience : Philosophical Foundation

"Work Experience is dominated by pragmatic philosophy as its aim is making the child capable of acquiring the knowledge for himself and also the skills necessary to deal effectively with real life situations."

— **Sarusk Mahood**

Work Experience is an important concept. It has sound philosophical, psychological and sociological foundations or bases. In this chapter, we are highlighting its philosophical foundation.

1. Philosophy & Idealism:

The philosophy of idealism has emphasized that ideals, norms and values should form the basis of every activity of life and education must seek to promote them. In ancient India, i.e. during the Vedic age, this philosophy dominated all aspects of life and in the Vedic educational system. The ancient *Gurus, Gurukuls* and *Ashrams* not only taught or preached the high ideals and values to their students but asked and motivated them to do a number of activities relating to practical work, manual work or physical work, as well as social or community service activities. In their curriculum 64 arts were taught which were actually skills to do activities releated to life which they would have to lead as *grihastha* (householders) after completing their education. These skilled activities gave them invaluable Work Experience which made them ideal and competent members of the society as well as successful householders, and members of the community. In all religious communities, besides imparting theory of religion and spirituality, the religious teachers, and *gurus* invariably motivated the younger ones of the community to do a number of manual activities which provided them with valuable work experience as they did with great enthusiasm and dedication. They taught many human and social values while doing the Work Experience activities such as love, cooperation, honesty, truth, appreciation of beauty, concern for others, respect for one's culture and religion, selflessness and sincerity. The Buddhist monks, Christian monks, the Muslim teachers, and even tribal religions personalities and then assistants internalized these high values.

All great philosophers like Socrates, Plato, and educators like Rosseau, Comenius A.N. Whitehead, Bernard Russell etc., therefore, laid great emphasis on involving students in such practical activities.

2. Pragmatic Philosophy

The pioneers of the philosophy of pragmatism, which had developed in the USA in the early 20th Century, like Professor John Deway and many of his followers, laid much stress on all those ideas, activities and their experiences which are related to practical work, useful work, cooperative work and community service activities. The project method advocated by the pragmatic philosopher like Dewey and pragmatic educator like Kilpatrik was a very promising method of education which provided wonderful work experience to the students in schools. John Dewey has written a lot on the need and importance of providing opportunities for such practical life activities and experience to children in schools. He firmly believed that:

"Education is not preparation for life, but life itself."

He emphasized on gaining experience continuously. In Russia also, a great deal of emphasis has been laid on Work Experience, technical education and polytechnic education.

The concept of Work Experience/SUPW is located in the philosophy of pragamatism. Its practical and useful activities and social experiences are there, which provide children useful training, experience, values, attitudes and a world view.

3. Philosophy of Democracy

Now it is the age of democracy. All citizens of India have freedom and equality. All have equal rights. All have opportunities to achieve vertical as well as horizontal mobilities. Children learn by doing useful crafts and other productive work activities, from which they gain some useful experience about the world of work and they get help in choosing their future occupations and career. While doing Work Experience activities in groups, children develop team spirit. They are taught through much activities how they should perform in participative democratic spirit. The teacher must a democratic leader. It is not expected from the Work Experience in schools that the children should be taught how to work like labourers on farms and in factories. Its main purpose is that children should learn proper values, attitudes and behaviour.

Work Experience seeks to bridge the gulf between the high and low, 'haves' and 'have-nots'. It is necessary, therefore, that children should be taught that the work of any labourer lacks importance. They should have respect for all manual workers and also learn from them. They should know about their life, their circumstances, the work skills and values and how they are contributing to the community. This experience will provide an invaluable socialization to them.

4. Philosophy of Reconstructionism:

This new philosophy emphasizes that we must be conscious and ever-ready for the reform or reconstruction in all spheres of our society. American scholars have greatly emphasized on the reconstructionism in education.

In our country, Gandhiji, Vinoba Bhave and several leaders had emphasized this. The Kothari Commission (Education Commission 1964-66), also accepted this valuable point of view. In Work Experience, traditional as well as some new activities have been included, keeping in mind this very objective.

Gandhiji, Vinoba Bave, Dr. Zakir Husain and the pioneering basic educationists like Aryanayakam, G. Ramchandran, Kumarappa, Acharya Kripalani etc. were idealists as well as pragamatists. Gandhiji realized the need and importance of craft, social, cultural and cleanliness activities, village service activities and laid down that they were the core components of Basic Education. His famous statement—"A basic schools should be the spearhead of a non-violent social resolution," had greatly enlightened and inspired thousands of workers of Basic Education. His companion, Acharya Vinoba Bhave, has written a lot in a very animated manner on the importance of *Karma* (activity/action/work) in education, especially in the context of the *Sarvodayi Samaj* (emerging Indian society).

According to Vinoba Bhave, *Sarvodayi Samaj* ought to be based on high moral, cultural, social and economic values, humanism, socialism, cooperation, equality, freedom from exploitation of the individual and decentralization policy.

5. Philosophy of Socialism:

The Indian State does accept the idea of socialism. All citizens should have equality, but not over law formally, but also in the school and practical life in the community. All should be encouraged to contribute to the well-being and prosperity of the community. They should be kept away from economic suppression and exploitation that exists under capitalism. It must be remembered by teachers that Work Experience activities ought not to be taken by students in the ways, means and spirit of capitalism, but that of socialism. The inner feeling, expectations, aspirations as well the needs for grooming personalities have to be understood.

6. Child-centred Education/Progressive Education

It must be understood that Work Experience is an indispensable part of progressive education. The child is the centre of progressive education or child-centred education movement. The children's welfare should be ensured, they should get solid and functional Work Experience from the activities they are required to perform in the school. These activities should match the needs and challenges of the modern society.

It is expected of the teachers of Work Experience that they should try to inculcate initiative, self-motivation and related ethical values in their students. This is not to be imparted as a bookish type of education. The teacher must not use methods of discipline which are based on fear, cruelty and retribution.

The famous child educator, Gijubhai, had greatly stressed this point that on children must be allowed to do activities based on their aim, with their own initiative and in complete freedom and harmony.

The National Policy on Education (NPE) 1086, appreciated the pragmatic philosophical base of Work Experience, as is clear from the following extract of it:

"Work Experience, viewed as a purposive and meaningful manual work, organized as an integred part of the learning process and resulting in either goods or services useful to the community, is considered an essential component at all stages of education, to be provided through well-structured and graded processes. It should include composite activities in accordance with the interests, abilities and needs of the students, the level of skills and knowledge to be upgraded with the stages of education. The experience would be helpful for entry into the workforce.

—NPE, 1986

6
Work Experience : Psychological Foundation

"The child likes to do things
Let him wash his own hanky
Let him fill her own cup,
Let him arrange the flowers,
Let her clean the plate,
Let her pod the peas
Let her serve the food.
Let the child act,
And act at her own pace,
And all at her own wish."

— **Giju Bhai**
Child's Psychology (*Bal Darshan*)

Judged from the psychological point of view, Work Experience is very sound. We all know that children love to do various activities. They wish to express themseleves through the various forms of activities. They learn by doing things themselves. Learning by doing is an important theory and method of learning. Learning by doing interests all children.

They love play-activities. All activities are treated by them as play when children are allowed to do them freely in a congenial atmosphere.

The main purpose of Work Experience is to develop the children in all respects. Child psychology tells us how the physical, mental, social, moral, emotional, sense development (sense training) of children takes place.

The children need to be reinforced. The process of socialization is of crucial importance. Positive as well as negative factors must be looked into the socialization process.

The motivation, interests and the capacities of children must be properly looked after. How transfer of training takes place is also of crucial significance in Work Experience.

3. Dr. B. Mehdi and V. P. Gupta of the NCERT, in their booklet '*Psychology of the Child and the Curriculum*' (NCERT, 1983) have rightly pointed out that child wants to create things himself and resents and protests against the force of interference of the teachers and elders. The child has four roles in his childhood.

The child has not only to acquire knowledge, but he has

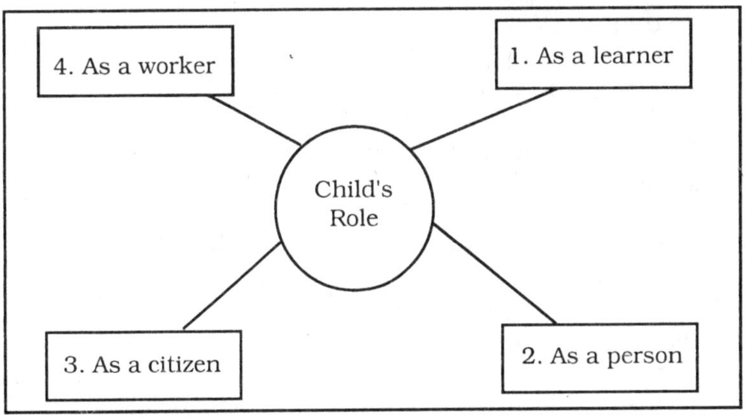

also to become a user and producer of knowledge. He has to become a 'Life-long learner'. He has to be properly socialized. He must be taught how to learn proper social behaviour from elders. His character has to be developed and the right kind of habits must be inculcated in him.

The child has to grow as a citizen. So he/she must know his rights as well as others' rights, and also his duties as well as others' duties, and how social harmony has to be maintained in the community.

The child has to become a citizen and adopt some occupation or profession in the future. Foundation for the proper work ethics, habits and attitudes must be laid in his childhood.

"It is a mistaken notion which many of us hold, that work is something different from what we call education and therefore, further feeling that it interferes with learning and hence, it is a waste of child's valuable time which have could otherwise been spend on his studies. The wrong notion about work arises when from the fact that we hardly appreciate the fact that work has its own educational value."

These psychologists of education have identified the following psychological needs of children

Psychological Needs of Children

Need for self-worth
Need for security
Need for love
Need for belonging
Need for recognition
Need for exploration
Need for self-esteem
Need for variety and change

Work Experience fulfils all these needs of children to an appreciable degree.

"Education imparted though activities relieves the tyranny of purely academic and theoretical work, it balances intellectual and practical elements of experience and helps the child to be curious and satisfy his curiousity while doing and discovering things for himself."

—Methow

In his book 'Talimi-Qudbat', Zakir Husain duly mentioned the curiosity in child. Children are very curious and eager to creat things with their hands in a free atmosphere.

7
Work Experience: Sociological Foundation

"Work experience has to be forward-looking in keeping with the character of new social order."

—S. Mahmood

Work experience or SUPW – whichever name may be used, is one and the same thing in the Indian education system now.

This is based on sound sociological foundations. A lot has been written on the sociological importance and bases of manual work, craft work, Work Experience or SUPW by Gandhiji, Dewey, Russian educators, Japanese educator Makaguchi and others. Since this concept includes social sciences also, great sociologists of education like Emile Durkheim (France), Karl Mannheim (Britain) and Herbert Spencer (Britain) have considered it to be a very promising social activity which has implications not only for the individual student, but also for the local, national and international communities.

We have identified the following main sociological foundations of Work Experience on the basis of our experience, thinking and reading. It is presented in the following points and diagram :

1. Every child has several needs—physical, psychological, social and cultural. The foremost need is to seek acceptance or recognition in his/her group. Work Experience fulfils this need. It gives him/her social purpose and identification in his/her society.

2. Participation in Work Experience activities helps the child to learn his/her status as well as his/her role set in society since socialization processes comprise of both these

Sociological Foundations of Work Experience

following aspects:

(A) Status socialization

(B) Role socialization

What is the social position of the child in the community and what role is he/she expected to learn and play to be treated as a well-adjusted member of the society.

3. Work Experience is not a theoretical teaching kind of activity. It is a series of practical work done by the individual in his/her social setting or context. His/her social participation helps him/her in having proper social interation and learning as well as in contributing to others.

4. Work Experience prepares the child to become an efficient and effective citizen and provides him/her ample opportunities to became a leader of the group.

5. Work Experience focusses sharply on the concept of 'dignity of labour'. It cuts at the root of the intellectual's shabby and highbrow attitude. Children learn to become broad-minded, cooperative and helpful as well as emphatic toward others in their group, community or society. There is a lot of educative value in a child soiling his hand in manual work and doing things with his own hands and on his own initiative. This gives him confidence to do practical things and become socially as well psychologically self-dependent.

6. Work Experience trains them in team spirit, co-

operation, mutual belief and a feeling that ultimately makes them tolerant and functional democratic personalities.

7. Several social skills are naturally learnt formally as well as informally while doing Work Experience/SUPW activities. How to do things efficiently and in a collaborative manner, how to maintain cordial and functional communication in the group, how to emerge as socially acceptable and autonomous democratic personalities—all these are well looked after by the enriched and well-executed programmes of Work Experience in school.

8. The Work Experience activities develop many social values like cooperation, mutual give and take, tolerance, politeness, love, truthfulness etc. in children. They develop proper attitudes towards work and life.

9. Work Experience activities are based on the ideals of social equality, justice and democracy. They go a long way in narrowing down the attitudinal gap between social classes and between the have and have nots.

All these sociological bases of Work Experience are significant, but we must take due note of these two important points also:

1. Most of the handicrafts or manual activities prescribed in the curriculum of Work Experience are very simple, trivial, uneconomical or unpaying and impractical.

2. Many activities like bee-keeping, tailoring, jam and pickle making, toy making, woodwork etc. are very paying. They should be included in the school curriculum.

3. In Japan, children in schools are assembling tape recorders, radio, electronic toys etc. Such activities are very paying. We should think of including such modern activities in the Work Experience/SUPW subject in Indian schools.

8
Social Services: An Important Component of Work Experience

'National unity and secularism, scientific temper and modernization of work culture and work ethics, and above all, a humane and caring society are among the pressing national goals."

—A.S. Kohli

Most of the teachers think that Work Experience means manual or craft work activities. It should not be forgotten that social services are also an important component of Work Experience. School authorities can think over as to which social services should be done in the community and how they can be done on behalf of students under the guidance of teachers.

For instance, the following social services can be organized by the schools in the villages, small towns and cities:

1. Cleanliness of the locality or area.
2. Distribution of medicines to needy patients in the community.
3. Organizing exhibition of charts on health, cleanliness, diet, diseases etc.
4. Organizing social and cultural events, festivals, celibration in the community/locality.
5. Helping the old people in the locality.
6. Rendering help to the poor and needy people in slums.
7. Organizing water huts for the public in summer season.

8. Rendering service to local libraries, hospitals, religious places etc.

9. Educating illiterate people and children.

10. Participation in rural welfare projects and activities.

11. Giving guidance to the poor and illiterate persons in improving their health conditions, habits, lifestyle, in campaigns against social evils and superstitions, etc.

Teachers can add many other such social service activities to this list of suggested activities. According to the level of education, suitable activities can be selected and done.

A.S. Kohli has written an excellent article on "Social Service and Community Development Programmes at School Level", published in '*Co-curricular Activities in School*, (1996) a publication of the I.A.S.E., Faculty of Education, Jamia Millia Islamia, New Delhi.

"It is the business of the school to set up an environment in which play and work shall be conducted with reference to facilitating desirable mental and moral growth. It is not enough just to introduce plays and games, handwork and manual exercises. Everything depends upon the way in which they are employed."

—Dewey, *Democracy and Education*

9
Curriculum of Work Experience

The NCERT booklet, *Work Experience in School Education* (1987), has very clearly and elaborately thrown light on this theme as under:

General Objectives of Work Experience

The general objectives of the Work Experience Programme are as follows:

Knowledge and Understanding

To help the child

— Identify his needs and those of his family and community, in respect of food, health and hygiene, clothing, shelter, recreation and social service;
— Acquaint himself with productive activities in the community;
— Understand facts and scientific principles involved in various forms of work;
— Know the sources of raw materials and understand the use of tools and equipment in the production of goods and services;
— Understand the utility of productive work and services to the community;
— Understand the needs of technologically advancing society in terms of productive processes and skills;
— Understand the process of planning and organizing productive work;
— Conceptualize his role in productive problems;
— Develop an awareness of social problems;

— Develop his abilities for self-evaluation of his performance.

Skills

To help the child

— Develop skills for the selection, procurement, arrangement and use of tools and materials for different forms of productive work;

— Develop his skills to observe, manipulate and participate in work practice;

— Develop skills for the application of problem-solving methods in productive work and social service situations;

— Develop his skills for greater productive efficiency;

— Enhance his working competence sufficiently so as to enable him to earn while he learns;

— Use his creative facilities for devising innovative methods and materials.

Attitudes and Values

To help the child

— Develop respect for manual work and regard for manual workers;

— Inculcate socially desirable values such as self-reliance, helpfulness, cooperativeness, teamwork, perseverance, tolerance, etc.;

— Develop proper work ethics such as regularity, punctuality, honesty, dedication, discipline, etc.;

— Develop self-esteem through achievements in productive work and service;

— Develop a deeper concern for the environment and a sense of belonging, responsibility and commitment to the society.

I
STAGE-WISE OBJECTIVES

Primary stage (Classes I-V)

At this stage of education, the objectives of Work Experience come very close to those of education in general.

The young children enjoy participating in a large number of activities in school, at home and in the community, rather than being engaged in bookish education alone. Therefore, emphasis should be laid on the development of good health, environmental sanitation and beautification practices through Work Experience activities.

One of the aims of education at this stage should be to develop awareness in the child about the world of work through visits to service situations or through participation in productive work.

The development of desirable attitudes, values and habits of work, such as the appreciation of manual work and regard for manual workers, cooperativeness and teamwork, regularity, punctuality, discipline, honesty, creativity, persistence etc. can be achieved through well-organized, self-expressive service and production-oriented activities.

Upper Primary Stage (Classes VI-VIII)

At this stage, children are sufficiently mature to carry out strenuous work with higher skills, which may require closer coordination of hands and brain. They should be encouraged to participate more intensively in production processes by undertaking well-designed projects in selected areas of human need, which will mark the beginning of pre-vocational* orientation to the Work Experience programme.

The children should also be able to relate their knowledge of facts and the scientific principles involved in various types of work. They should learn to apply problem-solving methods and be able to identify and use the tools, raw materials and equipments in a scientific manner.

Observation, manipulation and work practice should be the methodology to achieve the stipulated goals. The process of inculcation of positive attitudes and values should develop a deeper concern for the environment and a sense of belonging, responsibility and commitment to the community.

---

* This refers to predisposition, both to the world of work and intensive study of the productive process (inclusive of services and maintenance) as well as to the vocational education and technical training imparted at the post secondary stages, to which a sizeable segment of student population is envisaged to be diverted.

High School Stage (Classes IX-X)

This stage may be regarded as a linear extension of the upper primary stage in respect of aims and goals. However, work practice should assume greater importance. Though the Work Experience .programme, children should be able to contribute meaningfully to environmental improvement and conservation, reduction of pollution and development of proper nutrition, health and hygiene in the community.

At this stage, pre-vocational orientation should be clearly perceptible. As far as the curricular design is concerned, the development of vocational aptitudes or interests should be given sufficient importance. These pre-vocational programmes will facilitate the choice of vocational courses at the higher secondary stage. Even for those who opt for the academic stream at the + 2 stage, provision for enhanced participation in work would add a much desired dimension to academic education and produce better educated young people in general, which the academic course alone would fail to achieve.

II
Content of Work Experience Curriculum

The content at the primary stage will have three components: environmental studies and application, experimentation with materials, tools and techniques and work practice. At the upper primary and high school stages, the content will comprise of two parts, i.e. essential activities for the satisfaction of day-to-day living needs of the children, their families and communities and an Elective Programme of productive work and services, repeated practice of which would result in some remuneration in either cash or kind. The component of work practice is very important, especially for the elective programme of productive work and services at the upper primary and higher stage. However, weightages for it would vary from stage to stage. It is suggested that the productive work practice component at the primary, upper primary and high school stages should be given a weightage of 20, 50, 70 per cent respectively, depending on the total time available to this curricular area.

Further, the actual selection of activities/projects would depend upon the availability of natural, physical and human resources in the locality and the socio-economic background of the particular community. Care should be taken to see that adequate coverage is given to many types of activities or projects and that they result in the production of goods and services.

Primary Stage

At the primary stage, the Work Experience activities have to be simple and enjoyable. They should be in the form of environmental studies, involving observation of work situations and elementary processes of work, and preparation of handiwork from indigenous and low-cost materials through interesting, self-expressional activities. Activities should be so selected, that they help the children derive joy in giving shape to their imagination. Activities should also offer scope for experimentation with materials and tools, and participation in activities which involve helping the elders in diverse work situations, sharing work in group situations, as well as in fulfilling individual responsibilities. In the selection of activities, special care should be taken to select those that are suitable for their level of maturity, satisfy their curiosity and have the potential for developing desirable work and social values.

Further, each activity may comprise of three dimensions i.e.,

(i) observation of work situations and identification of problems;

(ii) participation in work situations and converting waste materials into useful or beautiful objects; and

(iii) preparing useful/beautiful articles in a large number.

Environmental Studies and Application

These activities should be such that they lead to the development of self-reliance in meeting day-to-day needs and to the improvement of the environment. Some of the specific self-reliant and environment related activities under various need areas are:

1. Participation in the sanitation maintenance and beautification of home and school under supervision.
2. Supply and arrangement of drinking water.
3. Joining elders in environmental sanitation

programmes such as removal of garbage, digging of drains and soak-pits for draining out stagnant water, and clearing of unwanted vegetation.

4. Observation of garment-cleaning and stitching operations at home, in a laundry, in a tailor's shop, in a garment factory, etc.
5. Washing of ribbons, socks, handkerchiefs, undergarments, towels, dusters, stitching buttons; and polishing shoes.
6. Helping elders in the maintenance of a garden by watering, weeding, pruning, mowing, etc.
7. Visiting kitchen gardens and agricultural farms, and observing traditional practices and modern methods of agriculture.
8. Helping elders in farming operations (sowing, watering, weeding, harvesting), in cooking food, in taking care of younger children, and in household work.
9. Visiting work places and observing potters, carpenters, *dhobis*, *pattal-biri*-mat weavers, cloth-weavers, construction-workers, tailors, bakers and confectioners at work.
10. Visiting and observing the working of a post office, busdepot, railway station, aerodrome, dispensary, or hospital.
11. Participation in different types of cultural and recreational activities such as celebration of festivals, puppet shows, folk music and dances, community singing, etc.

Experimentation with Materials, Tools and Techniques

These activities should relate to a variety of materials used for various work practices and should help develop an elementary level of skill in the use of tools and techniques. A list of such activities is given below.

1. Handling of materials such as clay, paper, cardboard, bamboo sticks, leaves, cotton, cloth, etc. for making toys and items of daily use.
2. Handling of gardening and agricultural tools such as *khurpi*, sickle, hand-hoe, watering-can, water-pipe and pruner, etc.

3. Safe handling of knives, needles, scissors, knitting needles, etc.
4. Acquaintance with and habit of handling various types of cleaning and washing materials such as soap-powder, soap-flakes, soap-cakes, liquid soap, soap-nuts, cleaning powder, etc.
5. Acquaintance with and skill in the use of materials for preparing meals.
6. Acquaintance with and skill in the use of colours – dry, water and oil – for making drawings, scenery, charts, etc.
7. Acquaintance with different techniques of making garlands and bouquets.
8. Acquaintance with a variety of materials used in making kitchen wares, such as clay, plastic, iron, aluminum, copper, brass, stainless steel, etc.

Work Practice

Students engaged in work practice constantly use their hands. After repeated practice, each activity performed by the children should lead to the production of goods or services. A list of such activities is given below:

1. **Self-expressional activities**: Making designs on paper such as ink designs, prints with thread, spatter prints, vegetable prints, marble paper, etc.
2. **Paperwork** : Making greeting cards, book marker, flags of different countries, standing animals, decorative pieces, geometrical models, gliders, floating figures, boomerangs, whistles, buntings, *phirkee*, office envelopes and postal envelopes.
3. **Cardsheet and cardboard work** : Making articles such as tumbler, funnel, pencil/pen stand, cardboard box, letter holder, dustbin, flower basket, file cover.
4. **Clay modeling** : preparation of toys including dolls and models, collection of materials such as leaves, shells, flowers, seeds, feathers, etc.
5. **Food and drinks** : Preparation of drinks such as tea, coffee, *neembupani*, squash, *sharbat*, etc., preparation of simple food items such as rice, *chapati*, *dal*, soup etc.
6. **Raising plants in pots**.

Upper Primary Stage (Classes VI-VIII)

Essential Activities

The nature of activities selected for the purpose should be such that they can be performed by all the schools offering upper primary stage education. By and large, the activities should lead to the improvement of nutrition, health, sanitation, productivity and economic status of the community. These activities could be selected from the following list which is only suggestive.

1. Maintaining cleanliness at home and in the neighbourhood.
2. Cleanliness and maintenance of the classroom and school premises.
3. Keeping sources of water in the community safe and clean.
4. Looking after sanitary disposal of waste material during festivals.
5. Washing and ironing of school dress.
6. Helping in the cleaning of poultry house/cattleshed in rural areas.
7. House decoration on special occasions such as festivals, marriages, birthdays.
8. Organizing community-service programmes for road repair, tree plantation and cleaning of surroundings in a village/slum area.
9. Helping parents in looking after younger children in the family.
10. Maintenance of personal and household accounts, payment of household bills (electricity, water, newspapers, etc.).
11. Making small purchases for oneself and family.
12. Coaching primary school children, including younger brothers and sisters who are weak in studies.
13. Measuring the height and weight of school children and recording them.
14. Preparation of charts and posters indicating causes, symptoms, treatment and prevention of common diseases such as malaria, influenza, diarrhoea and dysentery.

Elective Programme

At the upper primary stage of education, the learning and masteries of skills become more important than at the lower primary stage. At this stage, a large number of activities in related areas may be put in such a sequence that they assume the form of a project to be completed over a given span of time, ranging between one to three years. The choice of activities and projects should be such that the needs of the students and the community are met, keeping in tune with the maturity level of children of a relative group of 11 to 14 years. A suggestive list of such projects is given below:

1. Maintenance of school premises – whitewashing of school building, polishing of doors, windows and furniture, cleaning of chairs, and repair of school furniture.
2. Maintenance work at home – whitewashing, polishing, repairing, etc.
3. Care of clothes – preparing washing soap and detergent powder, washing of cotton and terricotta clothes, ironing, mending and storing of clothes.
4. Preparation of stationery items such as exercise books, practical exercise books, drawing notebooks, etc.
5. Bookbinding – stitching, cutting, cover-page printing, etc.
6. Repair of cycle, stove and simple domestic appliances.
7. Making of chalk, ink, duster, brooms, waste-paper baskets, dustbins for use in the school.
8. Cooperative management of school canteen.
9. Making of toys, puppets, etc. with waste materials for home decoration or sale.
10. Making of cardboard boxes, wedding and greeting cards, etc.
11. Plumbing – changing washer, plugging leak, fixing a tap.
12. Garment making – spinning, weaving, cutting, stitching.
13. Preparation of wall plates and decoration pieces out of plaster of paris.
14. Woodwork – making of nameplate, bookrack, wooden tray, side-table, etc.

15. Raising ornamental plants in pots.
16. Growing medicinal plants.
17. Raising vegetables in small pots.
18. Preparing plants through vegetative propagation – cutting, budding, grafting, etc.
19. Making of fruit juices, syrups, squashes, etc. for household consumption and sale.

High School Stage (Classes IX-X)

Essential Activities

The nature of essential activities will remain the same as proposed for classes VI to VIII. Only their complexity will increase by adding more dimensions, with a definite pre-vocational focus and on-the-job work. However, some more activities can be considered at this stage.

1. Use of bus and railway timetables.
2. Acquaintance with the working of neighbouring post, telegraph office, and banking formalities for opening an account.
3. Reception work in school.
4. Preparation and distribution of midday meals/snacks in composite schools.
5. Preparation of teaching aids and equipment for oneself and lower classes.
6. Helping school authorities in organizing exhibitions, picnics, tours, excursions, etc.
7. First aid activities like counting of pulse, taking of temperature and bandaging the wounds after their cleaning.
8. Helping traffic police in the regulation of traffic.
9. Plantation of shady/fuel/ornamental/avenue trees.
10. Preparation of family budget and maintenance of daily household accounts.
11. Acquaintance with common fertilizers and pesticides and their application with appropriate equipment.
12. Acquaintance with common pests and plant diseases and use of simple plant protection chemicals and equipment.
13. Handling farm animals for feeding, washing or general examination.

14. Preparation of soak-pit for collecting liquid refuse from the cattle shed.
15. Studying the nutrition and health status of people in a village/city/slum/tribal area.
16. Helping in community health programmes and enhancing the nutrition, health and environmental status of the community through door to door contact programmes.
17. Digging trench latrines during fairs and festivals and maintaining them hygienically.
18. Participation in adults literacy programmes.
19. Helping in childcare in crèches.
20. Volunteer work in hospitals and during fairs, floods, famines during accidents, etc.

Elective Programme

Work practice at this stage may take the form of projects with sequential activities relating to vocations in production or service sector. Each student should be required to take two projects, in and outside the school, depending upon the availability of resources and time. Students should select projects in such a way that at least two need areas are covered. The projects should provide vocational orientation.

A list of projects are:

1. Raising of flowers, vegetables, plants and seedlings in nurseries.
2. Repair and maintenance of equipment for plant protection.
3. Prefabrication of irrigation channels.
4. Developing plants by vegetative propagation – budding, grafting, cutting, layering, etc.
5. Raising poultry birds : (i) for eggs, (ii) for table purposes.
6. Making bakery and confectionery products.
7. Food preservation – making of jam, jelly, tomato ketchup, pickles.
8. Projects relating to non-conventional sources of energy—sun, wind, tides, biogas, etc.
9. Cookery skills.
10. Bee-keeping, bottling and marketing of honey.
11. Silkworm rearing.

12. Mushroom cultivation for consumption, preservation or sale.
13. Fish rearing in small ponds.
14. Post-harvesting technology and safe storage of food grains.
15. Use of bacterial fertilizers.
16. Preparation of milk products.
17. Plant protection against pests and diseases.
18. Soil testing and reclamation measures.
19. Preparation of stationery items such as files, file-boards, registers, writing pads, stamping ink, etc.
20. Tie and Die and screen-printing as commercial ventures.
21. Garment making.
22. Repair and maintenance of domestic, electrical gadgets.
23. Preparing electric extension boards for use in home, school or for sale.
24. Motor-winding as a trade.
25. Photography – commercial.
26. Preparing paper out of waste paper.
27. Preparation of decoration pieces of a more sophisticated nature out of plaster of Paris.
28. Mat and carpet-weaving.
29. Doll-making.
30. Hand embroidery.
31. Typewriting with adequate proficiency.
32. Stenography.
33. Preparation of nutritious snacks.
34. Preparation of a variety of teaching aids for use in school.
35. Plumbing.
36. Running a cooperative store.
37. Running a student's bank.
38. Running a bookbank.

Higher Secondary Stage (Classes XI-XII)

At the higher secondary stage, in the selection of projects, several alternatives may be provided to students. While some schools may provide a compulsory programme of non-formal education, adult education or several other projects in the area of community services to their students, others may like to offer certain inter-disciplinary Work Experience projects, which may essentially be subject based. These would highlight such applications of science or social studies which would be in tune with the concept of productive work or services. Projects on cooperation, leadership and entrepreneurship may also be offered in this area. The programme of the + 2 stage of Work Experience may be visualized as a linear extension of the pre-vocational programme offered at the preceding stage. In this respect, if the continuity is maintained from high school to the higher secondary stage, it may be conceived that sufficient pre-vocational experiences gathered in a particular trade can equip the individual to a fair degree, with regard to his vocational competencies.

Guidelines for the Formulation Adaptation of the Syllabus

Activities – Suggested, not Prescribed

The content of Work Experience programme is to be based on the needs of the child on the one hand, and on the resources available in the community, the facilities available in the schools in an area, let alone in a state or in the country as a whole. It is in keeping with this realization, that a suggestive list of activities rather than a prescriptive 'syllabus' has been recommended for the subject at the national level.

Besides including Work Experience activities of a wide variety in all the stages which, however, are not exhaustive, the suggestive lists also include pre-vocational courses as a part of the Work Experience programme for the high school stage. These are intended to help the states in developing a balanced curricula and to indicate the kind of content which can go into the syllabi after passing the test of relevance according to state needs and resources.

The lists have been prepared for different stages, i.e. upper primary and high school stages and not for individual classes. Therefore, contents under each item will have to be elaborated and specified for different classes. If an activity or project is to continue over a span of more than one year, the contents will have to be graded over successive classes.

Thus, the selection, modification, elaboration and regradation of content from these lists will constitute the process of its adaptation according to the needs of the states. In being essentially local specific, although a good deal of commonality is possible, the syllabi in schools and states should give ample scope for local variation in content, which should ultimately be determined by the district and local-level committees, comprising of school authorities, local community members, representatives of development agencies, professionals and employers, in order to facilitate the process of adaptation of the activities or the syllabus frames to the specific guidelines. The principles on which the Work Experience curriculum should be based, are stated below.

Specific Guidelines

Decentralized Curriculum Planning

Planning for the Work Experience programme should be a decentralized process. At the national level, only a suggestive syllabus frame for pre-vocational courses has been prepared to ensure relevance to the needs, resources and conditions which should be followed by the development of a model syllabus by the state. The model syllabus at the district and local levels, i.e. district, *taluka* and village – level committees should be set up for this purpose by including representatives from various government departments, development agencies and the public. These committees should work on local specific plans and programmes based on local occupations, needs and resources, which should be supplied to the schools well in advance.

They should also consider the feasibility of the provision of raw materials and the sale of finished products.

The syllabus outline, prepared by the NCERT, has kept in view the needs of rural, urban, mountain, and coastal areas. However, the outline is not exhaustive, and activities or projects found relevant to a state or local needs, should certainly be added.

Selection of Activities

The Work Experience programme centers around six areas of human needs, namely, food, health and hygiene, clothing, shelter, culture and recreation and social service. A balanced selection of activities in each of these areas may be made according to the educational potential of each activity and the facilities (materials, tools, space, teacher expertise, etc.) and time available for it. A variety of activities should be provided as far as possible, so that children can develop self-sufficiency in meeting their needs and discover their vocational aptitudes and interests. In the selection of pre-vocational courses, local traders and occupations should be given prominence. Moreover, a balanced distribution of activities over the three dimensions of Work Experience, i.e. life skills, Production and community service should be achieved in or according to their relevance at different stages of education.

Although the activities will differ from school to school, depending upon its needs and resources, there can be a programme of Essential Activities which should include regular and universal participation of children throughout the year. The other programme of productive work and services under Work Practice at the primary stage, and Elective Programmes at the upper primary and high school stages, should result in the production of goods or services, which are saleable or consumable at home, in the school or outside, and which will also provide motivation to students and their parents.

The purpose of Essential Activities is to bring about attitudinal changes, and to develop readiness for continued productive work. The purpose of the Elective Programmes is to give a vocational base to the Work Experience programme. It may, therefore, require repetition or constant practice, according to the time available.

Experimentation with materials, tools and techniques, and work practice. The first two are concerned with preparation for actual participation in productive work and services, and the third may lead to production.

In primary classes, study of the world of work through environmental studies should be related to the exploration of productive manual work and service situations at home, in schools and in the community through observation and enquiry. The focus will be on the variety of productive work and services around, workers engaged in them and the materials and tools being used. In the upper primary classes, the exploration of work can be more scientific and the social aspects of work can be further highlighted. In the high school classes, children will be expected to conduct work-study more systematically and to submit at least two reports.

Experimentation with materials, tools and techniques at the primary stage should be restricted to those that are plastic and pliable in nature. The end product may be creative, self-expressional work or some usable thing. Services should be such that children enjoy participating in them. At the upper primary stage, manipulation of harder materials like wood and metal may be introduced. Productive work in these classes will take the form of projects involving higher skills and precision. Services should also be of a harder and a more strenuous type. At the high school stage, related knowledge may be dealt with in greater detail.

Work practice at the upper primary level would involve the mass production of some items prepared earlier under experimentation and also the performance of some services which can be assessed in terms of some return in cash or kind. At the higher level school stage, one of the two selected projects should be from among the on going activities in the community, which require greater and constant attention. The second project can be of an ad hoc or temporary type. At this stage, the return from the work performed should be comparable to the market rate as far as possible.

In order to realize the educational objectives of Work Experience, it is necessary to follow the problem-solving approach. Children should be made aware of the problems related to their needs and the work that should be undertaken to satisfy these needs.

They should be led to arrive at the solution of these problems by discussing the materials, tools and techniques for performing work and services, and by undertaking work.

It should not be performed mechanically and must include planning, analysis and detailed preparation at every stage, so that it is educational in character. Improved tools and modern techniques should be adopted in the performance of Work Experience activities so that it leads to the understanding of a progressive society based on technology.

Allocation of Time

It is stipulated that in Classes I-V, at least eight periods a week, of 45 minutes duration each, will be allocated for Work Experience. In Classes VI to X, a minimum of six. periods per week should be allocated, besides the out-of-school hours for productive work and community service. Wherever possible, more time may be allocated to Work Experience in the school curriculum itself. Block periods may also be arranged, if necessary, for productive work, social service or visits to workplaces.

Facilities for Work Experience

Two types of facilities are required for the implementation of the Work Experience programme, namely, (1) physical facilities consisting of accommodation, land, workshop, tools, equipment, raw materials and (2) teacher expertise.

Some physical facilities as spelt out above will be required for productive work, for which resources of the community may be used. However, experience has shown that all students cannot be engaged regularly and continuously with the help of community resources alone. Besides this, the problem of road safety and transport are also there. Hence, schools should gradually develop their own resources, beginning with the provision of minimum facilities, a list of which with specifications, should be prepared by the state and circulated among the schools. Provisions should also be made for safe custody of materials, tools, equipment and finished goods.

Teachers for Wrok Experience

It would be appropriate to utilize community resources for the effective implementation of this programme. Although it is expected that all teachers should work as Work Experience teachers, a large number of activities may require specialized personnel. There should be a provision in this programme for the involvement of experts from the community. This will be particularly necessary to provide pre-vocational orientation at the high school stage. The involvement of all teachers in this programme would logically imply their proper orientation and training in this area.

Use of Community Resources

Utilization of community resources for effective implementation of the Work Experience programme is quite necessary. While it may be necessary to allocate minimum resources to schools for introducing pre-advantage, it may also be taken of the local business enterprises, workshops and work-centres for worksite and work training.

Development of Instructional Material

The nature of Work Experience, which is concerned with 'doing-learning', is different from that of other subjects which are, by and large, academic in nature. Therefore, the traditional type of textbooks meant for the subject areas or teaching of crafts will not be helpful in this area. The problem-solving approach and the integration of knowledge relating to different subject areas will demand a new type of literature for the guidance of teachers. Instructional materials in the form of curriculum guides, handbooks, source-books, manuals, resource-units and doing-learning units will play a very vital role in the implementation of the programme of Work Experience. Teachers' handbooks and source-books on the Work Experience activities and projects will especially be necessary in the immediate present, along with the specimens of detailed materials, such as manuals and doing-learning units.

III
Specific Guidelines for Implementation

The programme of Work Experience, as detailed in *The Curriculum for The Ten–Year School – a Framework*, published by NCERT (1976) on the basis of the recommendations of the Kothari Commission, has been implemented in various states of the country with varying degrees of success, at different stages and in different parts of the country. It has been implemented throughout the country under different nomenclatures such as Socially Useful Productive Work (SUPW), Craft, Work Education, Life Oriented Education, etc. By and large, the programme has left a great deal to be desired in terms of its proper implementation in schools, in spite of the policy support provided to it in Basic Education, and the strength of pedagogical foundations on which it stands. There is, therefore, a need to provide a definite structure to Work Experience, as applicable at different stages of education, so that it leaves less scope for varied conceptual interpretations and the programme renders itself more implementable than at present.

Sharing of Responsibilities

The policy statement in its paragraph on 'A Meaningful Partnership', referring to the concurrent clause of the Constitution, lays down the spirit and ground rules for its successful implementation. While the states have to actually execute the educational programmes, the National Government, above other things, has to ensure the quality and standards and monitor the educational requirements of the country, besides striving for excellence.

The center-state partnership so visualized, implies building up of greater capabilities by the state governments to meet the specific resource needs, administrative and supervisory requirements, training and establishment of desirable linkages within the state. For interaction within the national level R & D support system, a resource group of experts will have to be created to carry forward the work in collaboration with national level institutions, more specifically, the NCERT. Similarly, the administrative linkages between the concerned bureau of the MHRD at the national level, with the counterpart state directorate, will have to be strengthened.

State Based Resource Group

Since the R & D support available to the schools in various states has been diagnosed to be the weakest component for which a planned intervention is called for, considerable strengthening would be necessary, both at the national and the state levels in this regard. Depending on the size and population of the state, its cultural and geographical variabilities, and characteristics and such other factors, the size of the resource group would also vary. Drawn from other institutions on a temporary basis, on deputation or employed as permanent staff in the Directorate/NCERT, the nature and size of the resource group will be determined by the state government. While as an immediate mode of action, temporary arrangements may be resorted to, while for medium and long-range planning, more permanent structural arrangements will have to be made. The planning will be done so as to derive maximum support from the system created for the management of the vocationalization programme. The school system at various levels will work in close coordination with other supportive institutions, community, departments, agencies, etc.

Support at the National Level

The NCERT constituent units, both at the national and regional levels, will have to be qualitatively and quantitatively augmented to meet the needs and expectations of the state governments.

State and Micro-Level Initiatives and Actions

More intensive planning of the Work Experience programme will have to be done at the state level, separately for each state. The stage of development, cultural variability, etc. will place greater premium at during the micro-level planning and implementation. However, some guidelines will be available from the NCERT by way of sample curricula and instructional materials for various stages, as well as for programme organization and implementation. A few specific details, as applicable to each stage of education, are presented below to serve as indicators for local initiatives and innovations. A great deal of flexibility and adaptability will have to be interwoven into these guidelines to make the programme a success.

Primary Stage (Grade I-V)

At the primary stage, a variety of activities should be made available to the children. The schools can be provided with an open list of activities, with a great deal of variety suited to the intellectual and physical development of children. The Head of the Institution should exercise adequate freedom in selecting a set of 40 to 50 activities which should be conducted in the allocated time provided at this stage, which should be of the order of 20 per cent of the total instructional time. The choice of activities should also depend upon the interest of children and parents for its greater acceptability amongst them.

The proposed District Institute of Education and Training should be assigned the task of training and re-training of teachers of the primary stage of the district, so as to enable them to execute the programme of Work Experience in their respective schools. As a long-term planning, however, the curriculum for the pre-service courses for the lower stage should be suitably redesigned to train the teachers to take care of Work Experience activities.

In conducting the Work Experience programme in schools, the teachers should be encouraged and enabled to make use of the resources, both physical and human, in the community. In this regard, the proposed school complexes can also play a very important role. If each teacher is trained for five activities with the desired competence to have these conducted by children in a cluster of schools where there are ten teachers, there would be a pool of expertise to take care of nearly fifty activities, for the benefit of children of each school in the complex. Since all teachers of a school are expected to participate in the Work Experience programme, this type of arrangement will overcome the difficulty of skill competence amongst the subject teachers, which limits the execution of these programmes at present. Certain logistic problems may be encountered in the beginning, but these will have to be solved through local participation and involvement.

In case of single-teacher schools, which constitute a sizeable proportion at present, the teacher may not divide his/her students into five classes for the purpose of conducting the activities. He/she may constitute two to three groups of children at any particular time to work on the corresponding number of activities, in which older children can guide the younger ones in conducting the activities. In such situations also, the teacher may have to depend considerably on the community personnel to be drawn on part-time basis for imparting education in work practices. This again, is an area of local initiative and intervention.

Upper Primary Stage (VI-VIII)

In this stage, sequenced activities must be coupled with suitably designed 'Earn while you Learn' schemes, where the production of certain items could be undertaken on the pattern of the Madhya Pradesh Experiment. It may be cautioned that the 'Earn while you Learn' programme may not be made obligatory for all children in a given class, but should be made it optional for those who would like to benefit monetarily, by producing certain saleable goods. For this component of the Work Experience programme, one-to-two hours every day may be provided beyond school hours, when the work could be undertaken under the supervision of the school as a part of the total school activity. However, a time allocation of 1/8 to 1/6 of the total instructional time within the school should be compulsorily devoted to Work Experience activities by children of all schools.

The need for giving more intensive skill component to the Work Experience programme at the upper primary stage emerges out of the concern for a large number of children, who either drop out or opt out of the educational system after eight years of general education and seek their absorption in the world of work and services in the community, more or less on a local basis, migration not being a common, phenomenon for this particular age-group. In view of this the choice of areas of work should relate closely to the production processes existing in the vicinity of the schools and should form or provide the basis on the subject matter of study under Work Experience. The students should be made well-aware of one or more such production processes where they study various aspects relating to these production processes. For example, the cultivation of vegetables may involve not only the study and practice related to the cultivation of vegetables, but also their storage, preservation and marketing of the products of some extent. Such a participation in the productive activities the community would prepare the individual for better participation with greater productivity and it will also provide proper orientation to children so that they can identify their own talents, in regard to academic or vocational pursuits. Even for those children who continue their studies beyond grade VIII, the knowledge of the technicalities involved in various productive ventures in the society, would prove immensely useful from the standpoint of national development in a larger context.

For those students who continue beyond grade VIII, the pre-vocational courses shall provide continuing courses, but the course design should be such that it provides a complete package at the high school stage of education. The students may like to continue or take up new assignments after they complete the upper primary stage of education in high school.

Agriculture being the backbone of the country's economy, the list of Work Experience programmes will have to be fairly exhaustive in this area, not only to include traditional areas of crop production, vegetable production, irrigation and fertilizer etc., but also the components of the scientific processes behind high productivity, in respect of various crops, the role of machinery and farm equipment, the use of proper plant protection measures and a variety of services that could be organized for the benefit of farmers, for which earning could be visualized for those who offer such services. There has to be a considerable degree of flexibility in terms of relevance of the area selected for study. In view of the greater depth of such courses, than those at the earlier stages, it may be important to establish proper linkages with various developmental departments, the community, banks and industries.

Project activities in the area of business and commerce can also be introduced at the upper primary stage, which may cover store handling, running of certain business and office skills. Besides, a large number of projects should be drawn from the area of home science and technology, as would be appropriate for this level of education.

The Working Group on Vocationalization of Education (1985), has visualized committees at the district level for implementation of vocational courses. These committees may coordinate the working of an the area of Work Experience also at the district level. The concept of school clusters as presented with reference to the primary stage, would also be applicable to the upper primary stage. However, for this stage each teacher in a cluster may be given more intensive training in two skilled areas so that a particular school would have the benefit of expertise in nearly 20 areas. Each school may offer one to five projects, depending on the potential of the area, the background of the teachers, the facilities available in the school and in the community and other local considerations. Here again, the Head of the school should be given considerable freedom in the selection of activities for his school.

It would be extremely important to prepare instructional materials for teachers. Besides, a wide variety of modular materials should also be prepared to cover each course or project which would be for the use of students and would have details of theory and practice in an integrated manner.

It is important to mention that for this level of education, hazardous occupations should be avoided and safety precautions should be highlighted, wherever necessary.

High School Stage (IX-X)

The approach suggested for the upper primary stage should be extended to the high school stage of education, but with a definite pre-vocational focus. On-the-job work-site training should be given more importance at this stage. Such attachment programmes should be conducted during vacations. This will enable the students to acquire more intensive training through their participation in the production processes directly. While pre-vocational courses may start only at the high school stage of education, other can provide courses continuity with the upper primary stage. In programmes which offer continuity for a period of five years, it may be expected that considerable vocational competence can be developed in a student who would be in a better position for being greatfully absorbed in the community at an appropriate point.

At this stage, each student may have only one project of a pre-vocational course, but more than one closely related areas may be grouped together, if the time expected to be spent on each so permits.

It is important to allocate sufficient amount of instructional time in schools to Work Experience and to make provision for 'Earn while you Learn' programme at this stage and also in continuation with the upper primary stage.

It would be important to obtain the services of part-time teachers on a regular basis to provide the necessary expertise for theoretical and practical instructions in many of the technical areas. It would also be important to involve the employers and the consumers of the manpower in various related sectors and in the process of curriculum development at this stage.

Higher Secondary Stage (XI-XII)

The concept of Work Experience should be extended to the higher secondary stages of education. It would be a compulsory subject in addition to the language(s) and other electives which the students might opt for. The time allocation may be nearly 15 per cent for this curricular area.

Depending on the alternatives selected by the school, the provision of full-time and part-time teachers will have to be worked out. In some situations, it may be possible to involve the concerned subject teachers for subject-based inter-disciplinary projects. For the projects relating to education and community services, the entire school faculty may collectively take up the task of executing the programme.

Target Setting

Proper introduction of Work Experience as the backbone of the educational transformation, as visualized by the policy,

I. Contents of Work Experience at the Primary Stage

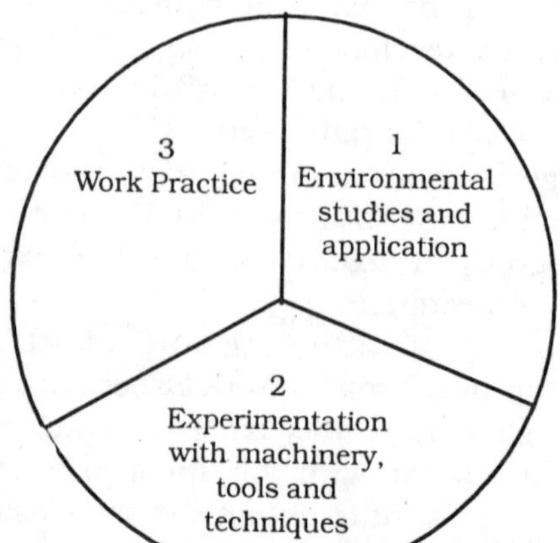

II. Contents of Work Experience at the Upper Primary and High School Stages

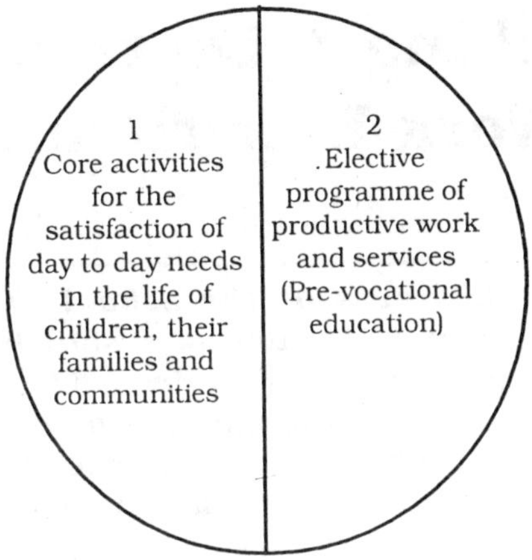

is a qualitative metamorphosis which will follow an evolutionary pattern. While the coverage of the programme has to be universal, the phasing will result in the acceptance and percolation of ideas in the classroom situations. The qualitative aspects will also exhibit a great range of variability and attainments, against the ideal condition that has been visualized. As such, all schools will be made the target for intervention in a concerted manner with the Work Experience being an integral part of the core curriculum in the framework (plan).

10
Teaching & Learning of Work Experience

> ***"It is the business of the school to set up an environment in which play and work shall be conducted with reference to facilitating desirable mental and moral growth. It is not enough just to introduce plays and games, handwork and manual exercises. Everything depends upon the way in which they are employed."***
>
> —**Dewey,** *Democracy and Education*

The schools must have proper infrastructure facilities for doing Work Experience activities and teachers must have clear ideas as to what activities are to be done by students of each class.

Three Phases in Teaching-Learning Process of Work Experience/SUPW.

***Phase* I**

Study of the world of work through observation and enquiry.

***Phase* II**

Experimentation with materials, tools and techniques

***Phase* III**

Work Practice

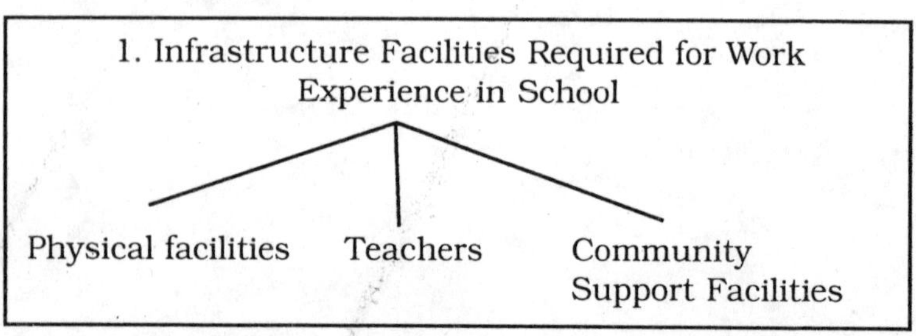

Basic Materials and Tools

In order to organize activities under Work Experience, some basic materials and tools will be required by the schools.

The materials and tools will be used by different classes at different points of time, as per the timetable. These will have to be procured by the school and made available to children, as and when required. There will be some consumable items, which may be replenished regularly. A bulk of such material is available locally and is quite inexpensive. Some of the items may be obtained by the children and teachers from the natural environment. Though most of the material is inexpensive, yet its judicious use may be emphasized. As far as possible, improvisation and mobilization of available resources may be stressed.

Activity	**Tools and Materials**
Personal and Environmental cleanliness activities, Chart on common diseases, carriers of diseases	broom, duster, spade, khurpi, dustbin, chart paper, sketch pen, gum, scissors, blade, mug, pencil
Artistic articles Decoration during festivals Earthen pot decoration Flower arrangement Chart on food items, properties of food	cardboard boxes, empty containers, glaze sheet, paper, gum, scissors, Abri-paper, kite paper, wire, coconut shell, locally available waste materials earthen pots of different shapes, gum, coloured powder
Chart on houses of different regions in India	natural flower, foliage, cord cutout picture of houses with various structures and forms,
Specimens of cloth of different yarns	gum, scissors, chart paper, sketch pen, etc.
Chart showing dresses of different types of yarns	cloth cuttings of different types of yarns, chart paper,
Charts of freedom fighters, picture of different festivals	gum, sketch-pen ready-made chart depicting dresses of different regions, picture cut-outs, gum, thin board, scissors, coloured pen, pencil, sketch-pen.

Preparation of Annual Plan

Organization of Work Experience in a school system, which is poorly equipped for such a purpose requires a lot of planning, with respect of scheduling of work based on availability of time, season, human expertise, raw materials, etc., for the whole year and for proper implementation. In view of this, preparation of an annual plan or scheme of work for the entire duration, class-wise and month-wise would be necessary.

For preparing the plan, the number of actual working days during the year or semester is calculated and the total number of periods available for Work Experience is worked out. This, however, will vary from state to state, as the weightage given to Work Experience, based on specific requirements, are distributed week-wise and monthwise. The methods and techniques of doing the work are also identified. These include individual or group work, demonstration, field visit, on-the-job experience, problem solving approach, etc. The entire information can be filled in the following Performa, which should be by and large ready within two weeks of commencement of the class work.

Performa : Scheme of Work for the Year

Class. . .

Month	*Week*	*No. of periods available*	*Activities to becovered with*	*Methods of doing the Periods allotted activity*
July	I			
	II			
	III			
	IV			
August	I			
	II			
	III			
	IV			
September	I			
	II			
	III			
	IV			

Similarly, details are worked out for the rest of the months in an academic year.

Teaching-Learning Process

The teaching-learning process in Work Experience has three phases: study of the world of work through observation and inquiry;

2. The NCERT publication *'Work Experience: Class III – Teachers Handbook'* (1987) had suggested the following activities for class III students. These specimen can guide the Work Experience needness of other classes to think of and decide suitable activities for their students.

Activities Related to Day to Day Life Situations in Different Areas for Students of Class III

Health and Hygiene

1. Informal discussions about the need for getting upon time from bed regularly. Keeping body parts clean.

Taking body exercises in the morning. Observing postural rules while reading, writing, sitting, standing, walking, etc.

Covering the water vessel properly and avoiding dipping fingers and unclean utensils inside it.

Avoiding touching of other parts of the body after putting fingers on blowing nose.

Washing hands properly after touching a boil or wound etc.

Observing rules of social hygiene like spitting in a proper place, putting handkerchief or cloth in front of mouth and nose while sneezing, coughing and not to urinate or pass stool near water resources, etc.

Keeping belongings in order and dusting them regularly help in maintaining the sanitary conditions at home, in school and in the neighbourhood.

2. Helping elder children in preparing soak pit, compost pit etc.

3. Enacting drama about hygienic habits by children, using mask and proper make-up.

4. Using safety measures against mosquitoes, flies, etc.

burning dry neem-leaves, coconut shells, etc. in the evening.

5. Covering food items.
6. Helping classmates in cleaning the classroom and arranging things in order.
7. Helping schoolmates in cleaning the school premises.
8. Participating in cleanliness campaigns in the school.
9. Participating in cleanliness campaigns outside the school.
10. Attending to persons involved in minor accidents, e.g. cut, burn, etc.
11. Helping family members in cleaning house and nearby places.
12. Checking younger brothers, sisters, other children at home and in the school from spitting.
13. Requesting classmates not to spoil the classroom by throwing waste paper and ink on the floor.
14. Telling class mates, brothers, sisters not to keep their bags, shoes, chappal, etc. haphazardly.

Food and Agriculture

1. Informal discussions about:

Food items consumed daily and their need for our body;

Food items generally liked by children and our body requirements.

2. Showing the different parts of plants, experiments to show that plants turn and grow towards light.
3. Singing in chorus programmes with others.
4. Working in the groupwork related to school dances, dramas and birthday celebrations.

1. Works in the preparation of posters by cutting paper, aligning margins, decorating or writing.
2. Writes group reports of excursion or visits.
3. Works in different types of group, i.e. manual work the *Safai* work, gardening and doing work related to production of goods and services.
4. Works in arranging and displaying exhibits during exhibitions.

Usefulness of *chapati, dal,* rice, green, fresh leafy vegetables, fruits, milk, egg, fish, meat, etc.

Overeating and underrating effect on the body;

1. Utility of sprouted grains and pulses.

2. preparing bed for sowing seeds.

3. Sowing of seeds and observing germination of seeds.

4. Watering the plants, observing plant growth, looking after plants, weeding out unwanted plants, grass, etc.

5. Protecting tender plants from hot sun.

6. Protecting plants from insects and other animals.

7. Observing birds, insects and animals that help in the plant growth and protecting from those who are their enemies.

8. Preparing for protecting crops from birds and animals.

9. Rendering help to elders in preparing mud *kothis* for storing grain.

10. Assisting elders in collecting necessary materials for preparing a machine so that vigilance can be kept on the crops.

11. Helping elders in preparing a boundary to the garden with the help of dry grass, thorny plants, etc.

12. Preparing a dummy of crow or human figures for the field, with a view to scaring birds from eating crops, fruits, etc.

13. Preparing, charts of harmless and harmful insects with picture cut-outs.

14. Observing seasonal vegetables and fruits.

15. Preparing charts of seasonal vegetables and fruits.

16. Identifying the fruits and vegetables that are useful for our body.

17. Writing names of seasonal fruits, vegetables and their food value

18. Helping elders in food preparation activities like peeling seeds, removing skin from vegetables, isolating unwanted articles from rice, pulses and washing them properly.

19. Cooking simple food items like, rice, *dal, chapati* and boiling sweet potato etc.

20. Preserving vegetables, e.g. peas, spinach, *saag, chana,* etc.

21. Preparing potato chips.

22. Taking care to cover eatables.

23. Protecting food items from cat, rat, dog, etc.

24. Giving fodder to the animals and food to the birds and pets—cat, dog, etc.

Shelter

1. Informal discussions about:

Various types of habitations for man, animals and birds (natural and artificial).

Special characteristics of houses in different areas-village, city and semi-urban areas;

Materials used in different types of houses—their advantages and disadvantages;

The houses found in different geographical areas for sunlight and disposal of smoke;

Need for making separate dwelling places for human beings and animals, e.g. goat, cow, buffalo, etc.

2. Collecting photographs or pictures of different types of houses and preparing charts out of picture cut-outs and writing captions against each.

3. Preparing models of houses with mud, straw, dry grass and cardboard paper etc.

4. Helping elders in repairing kachcha walls after rains.

5. Helping elders in collecting and bringing materials for making huts.

6. Making safety arrangements inside the dwelling, huts of animals and protecting them from hot and cold weather.

7. Helping elders in attending to minor repairs of *kachcha* roofs of huts to avoid leakage during rainy season.

Clothing

1. Informal discussions about:

Need for using clothes, and children's clothes in summer and winter seasons;

Care of clothes-protecting clothes from rat, insects, etc.

Care of clothes worn on special occasions.

Repair of school dresses on time.

Method of washing different types of clothes.

2. Taking special care of clothes while playing games, doing hand work, attending household work, cleaning etc.

3. Avoiding rubbing dirty hands on curtains, dresses, etc.

4. Washing simple clothes of daily wear.

5. Drying the clothes by properly spreading them in the sun.

6. Folding the dried clothes properly and keeping them

in an orderly manner.

7. Keeping the clothes at a proper place while changing dress.
8. Stitching buttons.
9. Doing minor mending of clothes.
10. Protecting woollen and silk clothes from moth and other insects by using dry neem-leaves and other such locally available materials.
11. Stitching simple clothes like handkerchief, napkin by *kachcha*, hemming, etc.
12. Helping younger brothers/sisters in changing their dress.
13. Preparing cloth toy materials for daily use, e.g. ball, duster, puppet, lunch box cover, etc.
14. Preparing jute or gunny bag asam with thread of saree border.
15. Doing thread, string, wool, leaf macramé work.

School Celebrations

1. Importance of National Days, Special Days, social festivals of national/regional and local importance.

Various ways of celebrating them in different regions and the stories associated with them:

(a) National Days—Independence Day, Republic Day, Mahatma Gandhi's Birthday, Saheed Divas, etc.

(b) Special Days—Mother's Day, Parent's Day, Children's Day, Old Men's Day, Teacher's Day, Women's Day, Children's Birthday, etc.

(c) Festivals of National and Local importance:

(i) National level—Dipawali, Holi, Dussehra, Moharram, Id, Christmas, Janmashtami.

(ii) Regional level—Durga Puja, Basant Panchmi, Ganesh Chaturthee, Goverdhan Puja, Raksha Bandhan, Ram Nawami, Shivaratri, Onam, Pongal, Lohri, Makar Sankaranti, etc.

(iii) Local—Chhat, Karwachauth, Sarbul, Marma, Nagpanchami, Wangala, Nanghkrem Dance and Shad Shuk Meinsem Dance, Beihdergbklam Dance, Dukpa Tashi, Chapchar Kut, Loosang, Shad Suk Meinsem and Shad Nonghkrem, Yao Sung Lai, Haraoba, Agalmakaor Achiroka,

Rongchugala, Jamegopaaha U.A. Bhogale Bihu Rangali, Kati Bibu, Batbon Puja Kheritpuja, Batsagn festivals of North East States, i.e. Assam Meghalaya, Mizoram, Tripura, Manipur, etc.

2. Collecting portraits of national figures from old magazines, old calendars and pasting the on the chart paper.
3. Preparing National flag, garlands, invitation cards, badges, etc.
4. Narrating stories associated with various types of festivals.
5. Decorating the school colourfully on the festive occasion.
6. Participating in discussions related to customs and traditions observed in the celebration of festivals in different places.
7. Taking care of visitors and invitees attending the function.
8. Enacting stories associated with various types of festivals.
9. Participating in folk dance and festival songs.
10. Participating in local functions and festivals organized by different communities.
11. Narrating with actions, the story of India's freedom struggle.
12. Reciting patriotic songs.
13. Singing the National Anthem with a proper accent and tune.
14. Writing a description of a festival day.
15. Helping schoolmates in organizing a community lunch.
16. Helping elders in the eatable stalls or shops of festivals.

Converting Waste Materials into Useful Articles

1. Informal discussions about locally available waste materials and their use in the preparation of decoration pieces and objects of daily use.

   Sources of the materials, method of collecting and storing the materials.
2. Preparing leaf plates, bowls, utensils for cleaning rice/cereals, etc.

3. Preparing broom, duster out of grass, leaf, twig, etc.

4. Preparing bookmark and rack for keeping letters/files out of cardboard places.

5. Preparing colourful kites, soft toys and mobile toys.

6. Preparing cardboard models of bus, train, bullock cart, etc.

7. Preparing *bagn*, hand-fans out of locally available leaves, grass, cloth pieces etc.

8. Preparing decoration pieces like cap, wall-hanger, flower, flower vase, etc., using different types of materials.

9. Preparing masks, puppets, etc. and decorating them with colour.

10. Dyeing clothes with natural objects like flower, leaves, etc. and making flags.

11. Decorating dresses.

12. Decorating earthen pots with various designs.

13. Converting egg-shell, fused-bulb, conch-shell, nuts, balloons into beautiful objects.

14. Decorating the floor with different objects.

15. Preparing simple toys with bamboo sticks.

Collection of Materials

1. Collecting materials from home and nearby places, e.g. cloth pieces, used container, old calendar, shoe-boxes, used socks, wrappers of objects, coloured paper, used ball-pen refill, used cardboard boxes, wool, jute, border of sarees, cotton, beads, used thread-reel, twig, zari, coin, cork, thermocol from the packing box, used greeting cards, used injection bottles, etc.

2. Collecting materials from nature, e.g. stone, pebbles, coloured sand, sawdust, dry grass, leaves, seeds, feathers, bird nests, bamboo strips, paddy, wheat, millet, shells of nut, coconut, flower, etc.

3. Collecting from work places, information and objects such as a picture, leaflet samples of metals and things prepared etc.

4. Arranging and classifying materials collected from different sources.

5. Collecting information about the objects collected and writing about the characteristics of each.

6. Keeping the objects in an orderly way in one corner.

Service to Others

1. Informal discussions about:

Need for helping younger brothers, sisters, neighbours children;

Need for mixing up affectionately with children coming from disadvantaged communities; Care of physically handicapped children.

2. Giving company and playing with the sick and old/ elderly people.
3. Accompanying old people to temples and other places of their liking.
4. Helping the blind and physically handicapped people in crossing the road, boarding the bus etc.
5. Helping teachers and schoolmates by conveying messages for them.
6. Helping teachers in classroom activities, e.g. arranging charts, holding things for them, bringing books, teaching-aids and other materials.
7. Looking after domestic animals.
8. Attending to visitors/guests.
9. Showing regard to people by rendering services to them and talking politely.

11
Evaluation in Work Experience

"A well designed plan of continuous, comprehensive evaluation, using worthwhile evaluative criteria should be prepared."

— Work Experience in School Education

The NCERT publication, '*Work Experience in School Education*' *(1987)* has suggested the following in regard to the evaluation of pupils.

Evaluation of Pupils

The entire evaluation in the area of Work Experience should be a continuous process from Grade I to the end of Grade XII. The evaluation should be internally conducted by the teacher or teachers of the subject and should be shown on the performance record of the student. It should take care of theory and practice in an integrated manner, but more weightage should be given to the evaluation of actual practical work.

Even at the end of the high school stage of education, external evaluation may not be the right approach. However, if the programme is likely to suffer in the absence of such an external evaluation, the practice of examining the students by external examiners particularly drawn from the cluster of schools, of which a particular school is a member, may provide a better alternative than the conventional type of external evaluation as practiced in several other subjects. The evaluation in Work Experience should find the same place of honour and significance as other academic subjects. A phased implementation of modern evaluation mechanism will also apply to Work Experience .

It is expected that in the evaluation of students will be given to development at the primary stage, and skill development will receive maximum weightage at the high school stage. This will have to be reflected in the weightage assigned to the dimensions, in terms of time and marks. It should be remembered that Work Experience is predominantly a 'doing' subject and, therefore, actual work performance should receive maximum attention here. Some of the important aspects of evaluation are as under:

A. Attitude towards work:

1. Dignity of labour
2. Respect for work and workers
3. Initiative and interest
4. Social commitment
5. Discipline
6. Co-operation

B. Project or practical work

1. Techniques adopted
2. Accuracy and finish
3. Cost estimation
4. Saleabilitiy of the product

Or

1. Social service
2. Participation in the activity
3. Organization of work
4. Leadership
5. Efficiency in execution

C. Overall performance

1. Inter-relation of the subject study with work
2. Preparation for professional or vocational studies

Teachers should keep systematic records of pupils progress in Work Experience. Apart from the teachers' record, each student may be asked to maintain his own record card as given below:

	Class	Section

1. Name
2. Work Experience area
3. Name of the unit
4. Unit started on
5. Unit completed on

6. Tools used
7. Raw materials used
8. Difficulties faced, if any
9. Techniques adopted
10. Cost of production
11. Uses of finished product
12. Underlying scientific principles
13. Assessment by the teacher in terms of grades and marks on:
    (a) Time taken
    (b) Use of tools
    (c) Use of materials & wastage
    (d) Finish
    (e) Discipline and group cooperation
    (f) Safe work habits
    (g) Utility of the product
    overall assessment
    grade/marks

Signature of the teacher

Date:

Students should make necessary entries in the card with the help of the teacher after completion of every unit of activity.

For internal assessment, a well designed plan of continuous, comprehensive evaluation, using worthwhile evaluative criteria, should be prepared. Assessment may be made and recorded after every operational stage of activity, project or its completion.

Self-confidence

I. The child speaks and reads confidently.

3	2	1
Very Frequently	Frequently	Rarely

II. The child works confidently, even when alone.

3	2	1
Very Frequently	Frequently	Rarely

III. The child plays boldly.

3	2	1
Very Frequently	Frequently	Rarely

Curiosity

I. The child shows interest in knowing about new and unfamiliar things or aspects in the environment.

3	2	1
Very Frequently	Frequently	Rarely

II. The child asks probing questions.

3	2	1
Very Frequently	Frequently	Rarely

III. The child observes keenly his surroundings.

3	2	1
Very Frequently	Frequently	Rarely

Cooperation

I. The child participates in group activities, when required.

3	2	1
Very Frequently	Frequently	Rarely

II. The child works towards the common objectives in group situations, when required.

3	2	1
Very Frequently	Frequently	Rarely

Suggested Tools for Pupil Evaluation

Observation Schedule of Self-confidence

S.No.	School Situational Behaviours	School Situations
1.	The child speaks and reads confidently.	The child: 1. Is clear and articulate in expression while answering questions pertaining to different subjects. 2. Speaks confidently in the *Balsabha*. 3. Sings spontaneously and clearly. 4. Narrates a story well. 5. Recites poems well. 6. Reads clearly. 7. Talks freely when he meets strangers who visit the school. 8. Answers the questions raised by visitors, etc. 9. Is not nervous while answering questions in the class. 10. Is not nervous while enacting a role in a drama.
II.	The child works confidently, even when alone.	The child: 1. Takes willingly, any responsibility regarding gardening and other types of craftwork.

S.No.	School Situational Behaviours	School Situations
		2. Demonstrates the models made by him. 3. Collects leaves and explains about them.
III.	The child plays boldly.	The child 1. Demonstrates newly learnt physical exercises and games. 2. Plays boldly different games.

Observation Schedule of Curiosity

S.No.	School Situational Behaviours	School Situations
I.	The child shows interest in knowing learning about new and unfamiliar things or aspects in the environment.	The child: 1. Shows interest in knowing about visitors, new teachers and new pupils. 2. Shows interest in strange feathers, nests, eggs, stones, leaves, plants, butterflies, etc. 3. Experiments with collected things, e.g. birds, nests, plants, etc.
II.	The child asks probing questions.	The child: 1. Asks questions about the nature and functions of unfamiliar things, birds, insects, plants, etc. 2. Asks questions about the collected things such as feathers, eggs, nests, stones, leaves, plants, pictures, etc.

III.	The child observes keenly his surroundings.	The child: 1. Observes keenly his pupils, their clothes, trees, plants, animals, vehicles, etc. when taken out of the class. 2. Is attracted immediately by the presence of new birds, animals, plants, etc.

Observation Schedule of Co-operation

S.No.	School Situational Behaviours	School Situations
I.	The child participates in group activities, when required.	The child: 1. Participates in group games. 2. Participates in group curricular activities. 3. Participates in group co-curricular activities.
II.	The child works towards the common objectives in group situations, when required.	The child: 1. Plays group games, e.g. 'Kho', Play of handkerchief, 'Kabbadi', 'Hockey', Kaura-Jamalashai' (Back and the Beat). 2. Participates works in the group-work relating to scientific experiments, e.g. Ring and Ball experiment to show that solid expands on heating.

12
Trends in the Teaching of Work Experience

The concept of Work Experience, propounded by the Education Commission (1964-66), was officially implemented by the Union Ministry of Education in 1966. Many educationists had hailed it. But several voices of concern or protest were also raised against it:

1. The Gujarat Governor reacted against it in its letter to the Government of India stating that:

* Ideally, Work Experience aspires to be a provider in polytechnics, not in village schools.
* Villages will oppose it, perhaps urbanites will also object.
* Workshops would be needed to conduct Work Experience activities. It is economically difficult to provide workshops in all schools.

2. The Uttar Pradesh Government had theoretically accepted this concept and suggested that it should be made compulsory in all schools.

3. In a conference or '*Nai Talim*' at Kundesuse, it was resolved that the concept of Work Experience should be carefully examined and then implemented with due caution, lest it may prove to be a flop.

4. The eminent Basic Educationist, Prof. H.B. Majumdar, Head of the Department of Education in Vihwa Bharti University, had pointed out the following in his article, 'Work Experience—An Analysis of the Issues Involved', in the *NIE Journal* (Vol. II, No. 3), January, 1968:

1. If curricular matter is to be related to Work Experience then lessons have to be developed properly.

2. Did Basic Education not have the capacity to fulfil those goals or needs which have now been kept before Work

Experience?

3. How would the forward—looking tendency be developed through Work Experience?

4. Earning while learning and self-sufficiency of education are ambitious and important concepts.

5. How will evaluation be done properly in Experience Education?

6. By fixing hard objectives in standards of Work Experience, both teaching and work will suffer.

7. The Work Experience will, in practice, become very shallow or an unweighty programme.

8. From where shall come the huge financial resources needed for implementing Work Experience in all schools?

9. Training of teachers in Work Experience is a very difficult task.

10. Without the production of suitable literature, it will not be possible to enlighten teachers and make them function effectively.

11. Will it be possible to take children to farms and functions etc., to acquire first-hand Work Experience?

12. How will articles created/written by children be sold in the market?

13. Basic Education had failed due to them is fortune of the administrative machinery. The Work Experience education will also meet the same fate.

14. According to H.P. Rajguru, Work Experience is not a productive work. It is only creative work suited to child's initiative, but it is of no economic value.

Proper foundations of Work Experience:

According to V. Laxmi Naryana, the following should be the foundations of the proper concept of Work Experience?

1. It should be treated as a core subject for learning.
2. It should be treated as laboratory or practical work, which is necessary in teaching service.
3. It should not be treated as an alternative to an intellectual subject.
4. It should be treated as knowledge of the ways or methods of serving tools and labour.
5. Its main objective is not to develop professional specialization, but it should develop occupational and

professional values.

6. According to the eminent Indian educationist, Father Fillela, in most schools where authoritarianism prevails, teachers and children are not given any freedom. If Work Experience is not implemented in the right sense, it would enslave, exploit, harass and torment children.

The Reality of the Presentation of Work Experience Today:

1. Most of the states have not, so far, organized any proper training programmes for Work Experience teachers of schools.

2. The cooperation of the industrial units has not been possible so far. The dream of procuring kits from them remains unfulfilled.

3. Institutions like IITs, Polytechnics, Vocational Institutions, Engineering Colleges, S.L. Institute of Vocational Studies, Bhopal etc, have not rendered any real cooperation to the schools in helping the growth and enrichment of their Work Experience classes.

4. The idea of joining farmers with rural schools has so far remined as a mere dream.

5. Only a few middle schools have good workshops due to availability of funds.

6. Small booklets and pamphlets had to be developed by the state governments to help the teachers and students. But this was not done by any one of them. Other publishers like Dehati Pustak Bhandar, Diamond Pocket Books, Small Scale Industries Department, The Khadi Board of U.P. etc have, of course, published many useful booklets which can be of a great help to teachers and students in Work Experience. But these books are not easily available to schools, especially primary schools, which are looking at funds as well as resources, on the part of this teachers and headmasters.

7. In most of the DIETs, the training in Work Experience is done in a slipshod manner.

8. Most of the schools do not have qualified, well-trained and dedicated Work Experienced teachers.

9. On the whole, most schools are non-serious about this.

This has recently been mentioned in one of the official

publications of the NCERT:

At the primary and middle school stages of education, Socially Useful Productive Work (SUPW)/Work Experience (WE) forms an integral part of the curriculum in many states, but the actual implementation, both in coverage and quality, leaves much to be desired. It has been observed in actual practice, that WE has degenerated into trivial activities in the school and in many states, the time allocation rarely exceeds 10 per cent.

The State Governments / UTs should ensure that WE is actually included as an integral part of the curriculum, that teachers are trained to impart the instruction and that necessary financial provisions are made. WE programmes are aimed at developing confidence and sufficient psycho-motor skills in students to facilitate their entry into the world of work at a subsequent stage. In schools where WE already forms a part of the curriculum, these courses need to be toned up, in keeping with the perceptions reflected in the NPE. Atleast 12.5 per cent to 20 per cnet of the school time should be allocated for the systematic implementation of the programme.

Appendix I

Minimum Levels of Learning in Work Experience (NCERT)

Work Experience, as an area of education, refers to purposeful and meaningful manual activities that result into either goods or services useful to the community within and outside the school.

. At the primary stage, the objectives of Work Experience come very close to that of general education. The main focus is to develop desirable healthly living practices. An awareness towards environmental sanitation and beautification of home, school and environmental situations are other important aspects of the Work Experience programme. Personality development, creative expression of ideas and thinking through various media and habit formation are some of the important aspects of Work Experience at the primary level. The programmes and activities under this area are to be designed in such a way that the learner gets rich experiences to work in group situations, with full understanding of the work, sharing tools and materials used in performing different types of activities.

The specific objectives of Work Experience are to help the learners to.

— recognize the need for keeping the body, belongings and surroundings clean.

— identify the productive work situations in home, school and in the locality.

— select simple tools and materials for preparing artistic and useful things.

1. *Seminar on Primary and Work-oriented Education*, New Delhi, NCERT 1970.
2. N.I.E. Journal
3. Conant, James B., *Education and Liberty*. New York, 1952, p.57.

— classify various tools and materials in terms of their usage.

— identify different service centers in the community and observe their functions.

— find out scientific principles and processes involved in various work situations.

— prepare beautiful and useful objects.

— take proper care of tools and store them in right places, in a systematic manner.

— adopt simple techniques for production of goods and services through repeated practice.

— exhibit good work habits such as cooperativeness, regularity, punctuality, respect for others, creativity and orderliness.

— appreciate the dignity of labour and respect people involved in various productive work situations.

The entire range of activities should be planned keeping in view the interest of learners, availability of resources at the local level and the learning potentiality of the productive activities. It should be ensured that the children learn in a joyful manner by participating in various types of activities through group

-learning situations.

The activities should be so designed that there is a natural integration between the academic activities and other day to day activities of the learner related to home, school and community situations.

The teaching-learning strategies should provide for using simple materials and tools efficiently. The planning and organization of community-service activities should be done keeping in view the maturity level of the learners and bringing the school, community and home closer to each other.

The activities should be planned in such a way that they provide opportunities to the learners to observe practical situations, analyse the work processes and participate according to their interest and learning level. On learning, participation in productive activities will lead to participatory learning and generate self-learning processes.

Major Content Areas

The MLLs in Work Experience have been built in and

around the following basic need areas viz. . .

a) Health and hygiene
b) Food
c) Cultural and recreational activities
d) Community services and activities
e) Work situations in home, school and community, and
f) Productive activities.

(From : *Minimum Levels of Learning at the Primary School.* NCERT, pp 107-112).

Appendix-II

Theories of Vocational Choice: Their Implications for the Elementary School Level

A) Sociologists and Vocational Choices:

Sociologists such as Caplow (*The Sociology of Work*) and Form (*Industrial Sociology*) have described the effects of economic and other sociological factors in occupational choice.

1. Caplow:

At one extreme, no vocational choice is involved when a child inherits his father's occupation. At the other extreme, occupational choice is largely in accordance with individual characteristics and is greatly affected by today's educational system. By insisting that the child makes various curricular choices, the school actually forces him to make an occupational choice at a time when he is still far from the working age.

2. Miller & Form:

Accident plays the deciding part in determining a person's life work. The expectations that parents, relatives and friends have for a young boy or girl greatly influence his or her choice for an occupational goal.

Implications for Practice at the Elementary Level:

It is important for the classroom teacher to be aware of the profound effects of sociological and economic factors in children's career plans.

B) Psychoanalysis and Vocational Choice:

The Psychoanalysts emphasize unconscious or internal factors.

1. Brill:

A normal individual does not need any assistance in selecting a career. He usually senses the right activity to follow and he usually runs into difficulties if he is given advice. "There is always some psychic determinant which lays the foundation for the later vocation and if not interfered with, the individual is unconsciously guided to express his sublimation in that particular form."

There is poor vocational adjustment as a result of selecting an occupation for which the individual is emotionally unfit. Career misfits are people who lack sufficient insights into their own needs and abilities, or who have been forced into a particular vocation for one reason or the other.

Implications for Practice at Elementary School Level:

This is not a currently popular theory. However, certain elements occur in the theories of Hoppock and Roe. The psychoanalyst view fails to explain vocational choice in several respects, e.g. different drives in different individuals may produce the same choice; there are usually a number of occupations that will satisfy the same person. If teachers were to accept the psychoanalytic point of view, as expressed by Brill, they would conclude that vocational guidance, including occupational information, is not necessary at any stage.

2. Occupational Choice as a Developmental Process:

Ginsberg and his associates believe that occupational choice is a developmental process that takes place over a period of about ten years. An individuals goals and values provide the basis for his occupational choice. The final decision has the quality of compromise—that is, to say, it represents a compromise between interests, capacities, values and opportunities.

The decision-making process can be divided into three periods –

(a) the fantasy, (b) tentative, and (c) realistic.

(a) The Fantasy Period:

A child's choice is based on his dreams and wishes, and it is quite unrealistic. The child observes adults engaged in various activities and he feels that he can do anything he wants to do.

(b) The Tentative Period:

It starts at approximately the age of 11. It is characterized by the individual's recognition of the problem of occupational choice.

(c) The Realistic Period:

This begins at about the age of 17. In this period practical considerations become important. Counselling is desirable.

Implications for Practice at the Elementary School Level:

Teachers should encourage the children. They should readily accept such statements, " I'll be the first doctor on the moon", "I'll fly jet". Gradually, the youngsters can be helped to explore the difference between fantasy and reality in occupational choice.

(D) Occupations are Chosen to Satisfy Needs:

Hoppock says that a student chooses the occupations that will satisfy his basic needs best, which he perceives intellectually or feels emotionally. Information about self helps a person to recognize what occupations will meet his needs.

Implications for Practice at the Elementary School Level:

We should help children in becoming aware of their interests, abilities and personal needs which they wish to fulfil through their vocational decisions. The more accurate the information given to each child, the greater the probability that he would make a satisfactory vocational decision.

E) Super's Theory of Vocational Development:

"Vocational development is an on-going, continuous,

generally irreversible, ordered, patterned and dynamic process which involves interaction between the individual's behavioural repertoire and the demands made by society, that is, by the developmental tasks. Vocational development is essentially a process of compromise or synthesis. In choosing an occupation, one is choosing a means of implementing a self-concept. One is actually saying, "What sort of person do I think I am? How do I feel about myself as I think I am? What sort of person would I like to be? What are my values and needs? What can I do to reconcile my self-ideal with my real self? What outlets are there with my needs, values, interests and aptitudes? How can I make use of these outlets?

These type of factors plays a major part/role in vocational behaviour and adjustment:

(a) Role factors, (b) Personal factors, and (c) Situational behaviour and adjustment:

Super has suggested the following five life stages related to the vocational development:

1. Growth stage : (Birth to Age 14)
2. Exploration stage : (Ages 15-24)
3. Establishment stage : (Ages 25-44)
4. Maintenance stage : (Ages 45-64)
5. Decline stage : (Age 65 onwards).

Implication for practice at the elementary school level, order of Vocational Developments in chronological order:

Preschool Child:

1. Increasing ability for self-help.
2. Identification with same sexed parent.
3. Increasing ability for self-direction

Elementary School Child:

1. Ability to undertake cooperative enterprise
2. Choice of responsibilities for one's abilities
3. Assumption of responsibility for one's acts
4. Performance of chores around the house

A child needs help at every age, in clarifying and testing his self-concept. Children should be asked what sort of persons they want to become.

F. Roe's Theory of Vocational Choice:

She (Roe) accepts Maslow's list of needs:

1. Physiological needs
2. Safety needs
3. Need to belong and to be loved
4. Need for importance, respect, self-esteem, independence
5. Need for information
6. Need for understanding
7. Need for beauty
8. Need for self-actualization

No other factor in a person that can satisfy as many of these needs as occupation does.

Parents play an important role in Roe's theory. A child's early experiences with his parents are reflected in occupational choice.

Implications:

Early childhood experiences to influence vocational decisions. Counsellors and teachers have a great role to play.

G. Havighurst's Theory of Vocational Development:

He suggests six stages in one's vocational development:

I	: Ages 5-10	:	Identification stage
II	: Ages 10-15	:	Acquiring basic talents of industry.
III	: Ages 15-20	:	Identification as a worker within the occupational structure
IV	: Ages 25-40	:	Becoming a productive person
V	: Ages 40-70	:	Maintaining a productive society, contemplating a productive life.

Methods of Presenting Occupational Information:

1. Using class helpers, e.g. one child can be appointed as Class-librarian, another can be designated as assistant master, etc.
2. Reading about the world of work.
3. Observation of workers at different levels by children on trips/visits in the community.
4. Bulletin Board devoted to topic "What Would You Like

to Be?"

5. Clubs, leisure-time activities.

6. Games : Edgarton's Research Observation : 70 per cent of children's games deal with occupations.

From : Morris, Wills, *Occupational Information in the Elementary School*, Chicago : Science Research Associates, 1963 : (Available in the NCERT Library, New Delhi).

(Summarized by S.P. Ruhela)

Appendix-III

Report of a Pioneering Symposium on Work Experience and Vocationalisation of Education (1974)

(Organized by the District South, Delhi, for Heads of Schools in collaboration with the Extension Services Center, Teachers College, Jamia Millia Islamia, New Delhi.) (December 6 and 7, 1974)

Foreword

The Delhi Administration has decided to implement 10+2+3 pattern of Education in the Union Territory of Delhi with effect from May, 1975. This decision is a far reaching one and efforts have to be made to implement it with the right spirit and with enthusiasm. In South Delhi District, a number of orientation programmes for teachers, parents and Heads of Schools were proposed to be organized to create a proper climate for working out this new pattern. Concomitant with this, was the idea to organize two days orientation programme for the Heads of schools, so as to enlighten them on the concept of the new pattern, its objectives, advantages and the needs at the present time. The symposium of Heads of Schools in District South was organized with this aim and it was very generous of the Extension Service Centre of the Teacher's College, Jamia Millia Islamia, New Delhi to have taken upon itself, the responsibility of organizing the programme at the Teacher's College and providing all facilities for the purpose. In this connection, special thanks are due to Dr. Salamatullah, Principal, Teachers College, Jamia Millia and Director of Extension Service Centre, for organizing the programme on short notice.

The new pattern of education is in keeping with the felt needs of the present and will also be able to meet the challenges of the future. Education has to be actively co-related with the manpower requirements of the country and in developing the economy. It has to serve the needs of the country during both, present and future. We are in a technological era and education cannot be complete without being technologically oriented. Work Experience is very essential to produce a complete man and this was the very core of the system of Basic Education propounded by the Father of the Nation.

We were very fortunate to have Dr. P.D. Shukla, Dr.Salamat Ullah, Sh. S.C. Chaudhary and Sh. K.S. Salamatullah who delineated the spirit of Work Experience and the current practices in other countries of the world in this connection. Dr. P.D. Shukla, who has done a pioneering job in the formulation of the new pattern of education, discussed the need for a change in the educational pattern, to withstand the current and coming challenges in the field of education in this country. Sh. S.C. Chaudhary, who is in-charge of Work experience and Vocationalisation Cell in the NCERT, discussed the practical implications of the programme and the criteria for selecting Work Experience activities in the school. His other colleagues in the NCERT namely Sh. Surender Nath, Dr. P. Raizada talked about the curriculum characteristics of Work-Experience and techniques of imparting Work-Experience respectively.

Sh. K.S. Bhandari, who is looking after the practical implementation of the new pattern in Delhi Schools, on behalf of the Delhi Administration, discussed in detail the plan so far formulated and the practical steps envisaged for the implementation of the scheme from May, 1975. He discussed the various activities listed by the Central Board of Secondary Education (CBSE), in providing Work Experience and analyzed them in the light of the objectives of the Work-Experience programme. Sh. Bhandari dealt with at great length, the methods of organizing and popularizing the programme of Work Experience in the schools and provided a blue-print for the organization of a machinery at the State, District and Subject levels, so that the implementation of the new programme may take a proper start. Sh. S.I.M. Zaidi, of the Teachers College, discussed the "Why, What, When and How" of evaluation of the Work Experience activities.

The work of orientation programme was co-ordinated by me as the Director of Symposium and I also presented a paper on the supervision of Work Experience, as it was felt that the scheme can succeed only if proper supervision and adequate guidance is provided to the Heads of Schools in general and the teachers of Work Experience, in particular. In conducting this symposium, I had the able assistance of Sh. J.C. Aggarwal, Co-Ordinator of the symposium. The team of rapporteurs did an excellent job with commendable speed.

I thank all the participants for their active participation in the programme and for their very intelligent questions and searching enquiries.

Gyan Chandra Vats
Dy. Director of Education; South

(1) Developing a Programme of Work-Experience

— S.C. Chaudhary
Reader, NCERT, New Delhi

The programme of Work Experience in the Union Territory of Delhi has to be considered separately for the middle stage (class VI to VIII) and the lower secondary stage (Classes IX and X). While the Education Department is free to develop the programme for classes VI to VIII, it has to develop the programme for classes IX and X, as prescribed by the Central Board of Secondary Education.

The Board has prescribed a variety of activities in the name of Work Experience for classes IX and X, e.g. Crafts, like Book Craft; Trades like Radio Repair; Fine Arts, like Music and Commercial arts; Performaing Arts, like Dance, and Community work. It has also suggested that the examinations in this area will be held internally, and will be practical and oral. The weightage given to the oral examination will be to the extent of 15 per cent. In prescribing the above mentioned programme, it appears that pragmatic considerations will be held supreme. Without entering into a discussion on the stand taken by the Board, it may be examined, how best the purpose of Work Experience can be realized within the prescribed framework.

The selection of activity or the activities for the schools

should be done very judiciously. It should be ascertained what personnel and physical facilities are available. Teacher requirement is the first consideration. The teachers should not only know the skills related to the selected activities but also be conversant with the pedagogy of it. Work Experience is to be used as a tool of education and not for simply developing manual skills. The ability to identify and locate problems, collect the necessary information for performing the work intelligently, select proper tools and materials for executing the work and use them correctly, and finally evaluate the process and product, has to be developed through the selected activities. For this purpose, it is necessary to plan and make arrangements for the work before hand, motivate the students for the work units, prepare them thoroughly before exposure to the experience and watch them when they are at work, for helping and guiding them. Their work has not to be evaluated by the product alone, but the process of work habit, formation of attitudes and values developed have also to be taken into consideration for preparing the profile of every student. For all this, merely a craftsman or an artist will not do. In case such teachers are not available, the activities may be selected according to whichever teachers are available, but then they must have been trained in the pedagogies.

Accommodation is the next problem. This may be the next limiting factor. Portable tool kits and hanging storing arrangements may solve this problem to some extent.

Supply of equipment, tools and raw materials will be the other determining factors for the selection of activities. Community resources should be tapped for this purpose. However, the interest of the students should not be sacrificed in view of the above mentioned difficulties and the easiest course should not be adopted to meet the requirements of the Board, if it does not serve the purpose. The occupational potentiality may be kept in mind in this connection.

Having decided the activity or activities, it is necessary to develop the curriculum for these areas. The document provided by the Board is not exhaustive for the educational practitioners. Neither does it give a clear indication for the day to day work, nor does it help the evaluator to evaluate. One should be clear about the objectives of Work Experience and the learning outcomes of the doing units. We should also know the methods of imparting the experience and evaluating the students work. We should also know what tools, equipment and materials will be required for imparting Work Experience. The curriculum should or include all this information.

The objective of Work Experience is to be able to develop work efficiency, work habit, insight into the world of work, creativity, versatility, and ultimately vocational readiness. The course outline has to be developed keeping the above-mentioned objectives in view and taking the prescribed syllabus as the base. This course outline will comprise a list of doing-activities and the related knowledge. Therefore, the entire course has to be broken into doing-units, which indicate the day to day work. The doing-units may be considered under the following heads:

1. Name of the Activity
2. Title of the Unit
3. Specific objectives in terms of the skills to be developed, knowledge to be imparted, habits to be formed and particular attitudes to be aimed at. As Work Experience has ramification into other subject areas, the related knowledge has to be worked out in detail.
4. Physical requirements for the unit-material tools and teaching aids.
5. Teacher preparation-planning, procurement of physical facilities.
6. Student preparation-motivation, discussion, demonstration.
7. Exposure.
8. Evaluation.
9. Assignment

All the above-mentioned work has to be done ultimately by the teacher, but the initiative has to be taken by the Department of Education or the Extension Departments. The NCERT can also assist in this respect.

The proposed programme should also indicate the much needed inputs for implementing the programme. This will be in the form of the necessary in-service and pre-service education of the teachers, the needed instructional material, tools of evaluation and curriculum reform procedure.

There is a consensus that Work Experience is to be treated as an independent area. It should be treated at par with any other core subject. As mentioned before, the main aim is to develop training or vocational readiness. In order to achieve this goal, the programme should not be confined to one or two crafts, trades or occupations, because the vocation of the students will not be identified before class X and even if it is determined, one may be required to change it for improving his prospects. Therefore, the programme should include fundamental skills and knowledge related to most of the occupations, or a major cluster of occupation or work division.

In order to identify these work areas, the manpower requirement has to be kept in mind and which has to be assessed. As the importance of non-formal education is being recognized more and more and in Work Experience particularly, we have to depend upon the community resources; the facilities available in the community should be explored.

In adopting this strategy, a doubt may arise as to whether there will be any difficulty in linking this programme to the subsequent programme. This difficulty will not arise as the programmes for classes IX and X are beginner programmes and feeling exercise is necessary. Also, a broad-based readiness programme will help to take up the work in classes IX and X readily.

(2) Supervision of Work-Experience

— Gyan Chandra Vats
Dy. Director of Education ; Distt: South

Talking of "Work Experience" in this hall of the Teachers College, Jamia Millia, today, takes me back twenty-one years when here at this very place, Dr. Zakir Husain unfolded his dreams of Basic Education and propounded his thesis of "Educationally Productive Work" for the first time in front of the then B. Ed. trainees. As a new entrant on the threshold of the teaching profession, I was enthralled by the startling exposition of the theme in the inimitable style and soft-spoken humour-tinged diction characteristic of Zakir Sahib. All of us understand the concept of Work Experience, which is no novelty for us. The only difference is that the whole fabric of Basic Education had been built up with the warp and woof of "Educationally Productive Work" whereas now, Work Experience has a very limited and peripheral role to play in the new pattern of education.

During the two days of this symposium, we have tried to discuss and comprehend the conceptual basis of Work Experience, along with its administrative, evaluative and technical ramifications. I would now like to put before you a few ideas concerning the vital aspects of supervision of Work Experience. It has been admitted by all, that one of the reasons for the failure of the Basic System of Education was the weakness of the supervisory and administrative functions despite Shri G. Ramachndran's wail, "Give us good administrators and we shall give you good Basic Education", in the Assessment Committee Report.

I begin with a quotation, "An efficient and sympathetic supervisory staff is almost as important for the new scheme as a well-trained teaching personal. Supervision is a fairly specialized work and we would recommend that a provision should be made for the training of supervisors to meet the ever growing needs of an expanding school system. Supervision should not be mere inspection, it should mean personal cooperation and help offered by one who knows more than a less experienced or less-resourceful colleague. Supervisors should be able to play the role of teachers and guides in the educational experiment. In order that the more important obligation of helpful guidance and leadership may be properly fulfilled, it is necessary that the load of unavoidable administrative and routine work should be as light as possible."

This excellent, exhaustive and exciting quotation is, as most of you may have wrongly guessed, not from some American publication nor from a renowned foreign educationist and not even from the large array of NCERT publications. This has been taken from the proceedings of the All India National Education Conference held at Wardha in December 1937, just thirty-seven years back and forms a part of the Zakir Husain Committee Report which, for the first time, enunciated the Nai Talim Programme of Gandhiji.

This quotation clearly earmarks the role of the educational supervisor. A supervisor has to be sympathetic and cooperative, as well as instructive and creative. A supervisor has to provide academic leadership and methodological guidance. However, the most important point that has been made is that "Supervisors have to be trained". So may first postulate for the supervision of Work Experience is that supervisors must be trained and must be fully conversant with the pattern, philosophy, programme and plan of Work-Experience.

The supervisor has also to keep in view the objectives of Work Experience and the supervisor should always try to assess the achieved quantum of objectives. How far has the school or the teacher gone in achieving the objectives set for a particular Work Experience programme, is one aspect of a supervisory practice, but what is more important and needs deeper probe, is the search for reasons that have held up the total achievement. Of still greater significance, is the need to devise ways and means to shorten the gap between objectives setforth and achieved. This three-dimensional approach in supervision is the corner stone of all supervisory practices.

Supervision of Work Experience would necessitate, on the part of the supervisor, a thorough knowledge of the processes involved, both at the theoretical as well as at the practical level. Then and then alone, shall he or she be able to provide guidance in the process and in evaluating the quality of the outcome. The objectives of the programme include intangibles also. They are:

(i) to inculcate in students, the spirit of modernization and innovation.

(ii) to develop a sense of self-reliance.

(iii) to develop respect and love for manual work.

(iv) to develop useful personality traits such as co-operativeness, hard work, rational enquiry, commitment to social welfare, etc.

These intangibles can be measured through keen observation over a period of time, through behavioural observation techniques. A supervisor has to take note of attitudinal changes through commutative records and by administering attitude testing batteries. The supervision will have to be thorough, intensive and time consuming. Thus, referring back again to the quotation with which I started this talk, it will be essential to put a smaller number of schools under one Supervisor and to free him to a large extent, from routine office work. He will instantly be on the move and will also have to organize a number of in-service training programmes for teachers, both of a short duration as well as of larger one. He will himself need in-service training form time to time and also get opportunities to meet his colleagues and give new in insights and expertise through mutual discussion and exchange of experiences. He will be required to keep a profile of every teacher working in his area and to maintain a chart of his progressive professional growth, vis-à-vis the objectives of Work Experience.

It is through coincidence, that the institution which pioneered the work in Basic Education in the country has been chosen as the first venue for a symposium of principals, for the implementation of Work Experience.

(3) Organization of Work Experience in Delhi Schools Under 10+2+3 Pattern of Education

—K.S. Bhandari
Dy. Director of Education (Science), Delhi Adm.

The task of introduction of Work Experience as a subject from classes I to X, can be divided according to the new structure as under:

(a) Work Experience at Primary stage I-V. (b) Work Experience at Middle stage VI-VIII. (c) Work Experience at Secondary stage IX-X.

It appears that the network of all the activities under Work Experience will be interconnected and well-graded according to the various processes involved from classes I to X. Its introduction at Primary and middle stages of schools will not be as difficult as its introduction at the secondary stage, particularly from class IX, when being introduced from May 1975.

It may be noted that the organization of Work Experience programme at any level, should be such that it links to technology, industrialization, application of science to productive processes and situations including agriculture.

Organization of Work Experience at various levels

State Level : Directorate of Education with its Academic Wing (a) Science and TV Branch (b) Science Centres (c) State

Institute of Education can plan out the schemes, thrash out its various aspects, its execution, taking mainly in service training of certain sections of teachers and provide all necessary help at the District, Zonal and Institutional levels in the preparation of various instructional materials.

District Level : At this level, the constitution of the following committee is suggested:

Dy. Director of Education

One Officer : Education Officer of the Science Centre, the S.I.E.

One Officer, Six Subject (One or Two)

Extn. Service Deptt. Representatives Distt. PTAs

Functions : The committee will sort out various problems and take further action for the organization of Work Experience.

(i) Adjustment of surplus teachers, requirement of new teachers, laboratory assistants, and work assistants.

(ii) Space adjustment, requirements of fabricated structures, tents and buildings.

(iii) Requirement of material equipment according to the activities selected.

(iv) Dissemination of the good points of the scheme, motivating and mobilizing favourable opinions at the district level.

(v) Devising ways and means to have more productivity and proper disposal.

Similar committee sat the zonal and institutional level can be formed with the Education Officer and Principal respectively as Chairman.

Subject Level Organization : This is another important aspect where the teacher or the guiding agency must be made aware, that whenever any activity is organized at the subject level, he/she should seek the help of the other school teachers, whereever possible.

Methods of organization : For Work Experience Programme, in addition to the guidance and training to be provided by the Science Branch, Science centres and S.I.E., the following methods may also be considered.

(i) PTAs at District, Zonal and School levels may be involved.

(ii) **Mass Media :** Radio and TV may be used for motivating public opinion, training teachers and providing situations where students are encouraged.

(iii) **Subject Teacher Association :** Teacher Association in each related subject will be of great help, in making it a great success.

(iv) **Extension Service Department :** Useful work can be done through the Extension Service Department by putting all agencies together for organizing in-service training programmes.

(v) Utilizing various institutions having necessary facilities.

(vi) Through other subjects in the schools itself (Project Method).

Other Suggestions:

1. A child may be required wherever possible, to bring some raw material from his/her home for producing a suitable product, which is most likely to be appreciated by the community, school and the child. This will help to motivate parents and boost their involvement in Work Experience Activities.
2. To make the Work Experience Programmes a great success and achieve its objectives. It may be observed that each child throughout the school stage obtains some experience of both industrial and agriculture production, or related aspects.
3. Efforts may be made to make each institution a nucleus of the community by providing it all possible assistance in the maintenance of its household goods and related materials. This will help to create an atmosphere of scientific literacy, which in the long run, will benefit the nation's economy.
4. Assessment.
5. Conclusion and Recommendations

(4) **Conceptual basis of Work Experience**

—Dr. Salamatullah

1. Education is complete only when both body and mind work together in an integrated number.
2. All productive work, which helps in fulfilling the essential needs of life is Work Experience.
3. All experience that is gained through crafts is Work Experience.

4. Work Experience should form an integral part of all intellectual programmes. Similarly, all intellectual programmes must form an integral part of Work Experience.

5. Work Experience is an essential part of school work. It would not be appropriate to confine it only to work on a farm or in the factory.

6. Provision of Work Experience activities is related to the social system of a country. For example, in GDR, farms or factories are attached with schools, but in India they will have to be provided in schools. Perhaps here, private enterprises may be reluctant to cooperate with educational institutions, in providing training to the students.

7. Provision of Work Experience on a large-scale will have to be made in our schools.

8. Work Experience Programmes should not be down-graded in school programmes.

9. Work Experience Programmes should be treated at par with other school programmes.

(5) **Curriculum characteristics of Work Experience**

—Sh. Surendera Nath

1. Work Experience consists of two words, i.e. work and experience. We must provide experience to the students in the world of work.

2. Work Experience may be divided into various sub-divisions – for example Agriculture, Technology, Commerce and Trade, Home Science, etc.

3. Three processes are involved in Work Experience:

(i) Production process.

(ii) Maintenance process.

(iii) Technology process.

4. Surveys for finding out the areas of Work Experience will have to be carried out.

5. Future needs would have to be visualized for taking up experiences.

Objective of Work Experience programme

1. To keep the potential school-leavers.

2. To assist the students in making occupational choices.

3. To provide first-hand experience to students.

4. To provide opportunities to the students to apply knowledge gained in the classroom to real life situations.

5. To develop specific occupational knowledge or skills.

Characteristics of Work-Experience

1. Work Experience Programme should from a part of the school programme.
2. All the work that the students do should be supervised.
3. Work Experience provided, should be socially useful.
4. School must contact the potential employers.
5. Students should not be exploited for doing manual labour.
6. Credit should be given to the students for work.

(6) **Developing a Programme on Work-Experience**

— Sh. S.C. Chaudhary

1. The Programme of Work Experience should be selected in a school very judiciously. The feasibility of the activities, in terms of accommodation, equipment etc. should be taken into consideration.

2. Teachers should be selected very carefully. They should not only know the skills related to the selected activities, but should also be conversant with the pedagogies.

3. For all of this, merely a craftsman or an artist will not do. In case such teachers are not available, activities may be selected according to whichever teachers are available, but then they must be trained in the pedagogies.

4. The objective of Work Experience is to develop work habits on insight into the world of work, creativity, versatility, and ultimately, vocational readiness.

5. There is a consensus that Work Experience is not to be treated as an independent area. It should be treated at par with any other core subject.

(7) · **Techniques of Imparting Work Experience**

— Dr. P. Raizada

Criteria for the selection of a Method

1. The method should be considered in terms of the aims of teaching.

2. The interest and enthusiasm to learn skills should be aroused and maintained in the students.

3. Use of audio-visual aids should be invariably made while teaching.

4. The method should be dynamic and not static.

5. Demonstrations of devices, short time drills, check sheet, timed drills, motivation devices, should form a part of teaching.

6. Skills should be developed in a correlated and an integrated manner, with clear knowledge and understanding.

Principles of Skill Building

1. Principle of Correct Technique
2. Principle of Variety
3. Principle of Planning in advance
4. Principle of Demonstrated teaching
5. Principle of Motivation
6. Principle of Individual differences
7. Principle of Cooperation
8. Principle of Automatization

Methods of Teaching

1. Apprenticeship Method
2. Demonstration Method
3. Project Method
4. Problem Method
5. Laboratory Method
6. Unit Method
7. Assignment Method

(8) Evaluating Work Experience

— S.I.M. Zaidi

1. Evaluation—what for : From the point of view of the modern concept of evaluation, the most important function of evaluation in Work Experience, should be to provide the student and his teacher with knowledge of results of their endeavours. It should not be linked with the question of promotion to the higher grade.

2. What is to be evaluated? Any programme of Work-Experience comprises certain activities, leading to certain results. Hence, both the process, as well as the end-results of work, will have to be evaluated. The end-results may be in the form of goods produced, tasks performed or certain socially desirable attituds inculcated in the students.

3. Who should evaluate? The responsibility of evaluating the performance of students should mainly be that of the teacher under whose charge the students undertake a work experience project.

4. When to evaluate? Evaluation during the very process of performing a job is essential.

5. How to evaluate? A nine-point evaluation scale would be more appropriate. Use of certain agreed description categories like, "satisfactory", "superior", "excellent" and "exceptional" on the positive side and "had an experience of performing such and such job" on the negative side, may serve as a suitable alternative.

(9) Organization of Work Experience

—K.S. Bhandari

Characteristics of Work Experience as a subject:

1. It appears that the net work of all the activities under Work Experience will be interconnected and well-graded, according to the various processes involved from classes I to X and its introduction at primary and middle stages will not be as difficult as its introduction at the secondary stage.

2. Categorization of Work Experience Activities:

(a) Science based activities
(b) Agriculture based activities
(c) Domestic Science based activities
(d) Craft based activities
(e) Commerce and Drawing and Art based activities
(f) Music and Fine Arts based activities

3. Organization of Work Experience Machinery at three levels.

1. State level
2. District level
3. Subject level

4. Methods of organization and Popularizing Work Experience Programme.

1. PTAs
2. Radio and TV
3. Subject Teacher Association
4. Extension Service Department
5. Institutions having facilities

6. Project and cooperative methods involving various school subjects.

(10) Supervision of Work Experience

—Shri Gyan Chandra Vats.

1. Supervisors should be able to play the role of teachers and guides in the educational experiment.
2. First postulate for the supervision of Work Experience is that supervisors must be trained and must be fully conversant with the pattern, philosophy, programme and plan of Work Experience.
3. Supervisor has also to keep in view the objectives of Work Experience and the supervisor should always try to assess the achieved quantum of objectives.
4. Supervision of Work Experience would necessitate on the part of the supervisor, a thorough knowledge of the processes involved, both at the theoretical as well as at the practical level.
5. Supervision will have to be thorough, intensive and time consuming.
6. Supervisor will be required to keep a profile of every teacher working in this area and to maintain a chart of his progressive professional growth, vis-à-vis the objectives of Work Experience.

(11) Operational Plan of Implementing the Programme of Work Experience and Programme of Vocationalization of Education

—Shri S.C. Chaudhry

1. For developing the operational plan, it may be necessary to identify the roles of the Institutions and the individuals concerned in the operational plan.
2. Implementation of the programme of Work Experience and vocationalization of Education involves cooperation of other developmental departments and agencies. It is necessary to maintain a liaison between these organizations. This has to be done at the official level.
3. For all this, it may be necessary to develop an infrastructure in the department, at the level of voluntary agencies and extension departments.

(12) Conceptual Basis of Vocationalization of Secondary Education (Higher Secondary Stage).

—Dr. P.D. Shukla

1. History of the curriculum development throughout the ages, makes it imperative that the present curriculum must be technologically oriented.
2. The economic development of the country requires that the curriculum should be vocationalized.
3. Curriculum should be vocationalized to meet the manpower requirement of the country.
4. Curriculum should be vocationalized to provide employment.
5. Vocationalization is an integral part of life. The curriculum, therefore, should be vocationalized.

List of the Work Experience recommended by the Central Board of Secondary Education, Delhi to be introdueed in IX class of 10 + 2 + 3 pattern of Education, to be introduced in 1975.

S.No.	Name
1.	Electric gadgets : their servicing & maintenance
2.	Electronics – Radio mechanism
3.	Basic engineering craft studies (Mech)
4.	Photography
5.	Maintenance & repair of house hold gadgets
6.	Gardening
7.	Fishery
8.	Agriculture
9.	Bee-keeping
10.	Poultry
11.	Seri-culture
12.	Lac-culture
13.	Seed production
14.	Bakery & confectionery
15.	Meal-planning, preparation & preservation
16.	Toy-making & house hold accessories
17.	Tailoring, Embroidery & care of clothing
18.	Music (Instrumental)
19.	Music (Vocal)
20.	Music (Percussion instruments)
21.	Folk dances
22.	Theatre craft

23. Puppetry
24. Maintenance & repair of musical instruments
25. Block printing, batik painting, tie & dye
26. Designing, dyeing & printing
27. Commercial art
28. Sculpture
29. Spinning & weaving
30. Cane & bamboo work
31. Typewriting (English)
32. Typewriting (Hindi)
33. Masonary work
34. Leather work
35. Plastics
36. Penciling
37. Manufacturing of sports goods
38. Pottery
39. Clay modeling & papier mache
40. Paper craft & papier mache
41. Basic engineering (Wood work)
42. Book craft

Appendix-IV

List of Waste Materials Which May be Uused in Low-cost Toy-making

Waste Materials in Rural Areas

Leaves • Seeds • Dried vegetables • Jowar stalk • Bamboo sticks • Bark of trees like date palms • Coconut shells • Groundnut shells • Dried beans • Corn cobs • Tree twigs • Sea shells • Clay • Straw • Broken clay pots, pans and brick pieces • Stones and pebbles • Old clothe pieces, Sand • Fibres of all varieties.

Waste Materials in Urban Areas

Nails • Paste tubes and their caps • Empty bottles, tins plastic and iron wires • Cardboard • Bottle corks • Waste papers • Bottle straws • Sand papers • Leaves • Ropes • Waste cloth cutting • Wool • Thread • Ice cream cups and spoons • Plastic glasses • Buttons • Used plastic bottles • Cold drink-caps • Used dusters • Empty chalk boxes • Electric switches • Broken iron pipes • Carpenter's cuttings • Sweets wrappers • Used ballpens and their used refills • Paper cutting • Waste Bobbins pulp • Board packages • Corrugated papers • Metal cuttings • Screws, nuts and bolts • Milk bottle caps • Cans • Jute packing leftovers • Plastic/ Thermocol packing • Rubber-band strips • Tyres • Empty cigarette packings • Big spools • Small spools (reeds) • Clay • Wood • Seeds • Shells • Pebbles • Leaves • Fruits • Wooden pieces.

Annexure V

Kurukshetra University B.Ed. Syllabus

Work Education & Work Experience Objectives

The purpose of providing Work Education & Work Experience to B.Ed. students is to improve the general efficiency of pupil teachers and enable them to perform better in their school,

To enable the teacher trainees to:

1. Explain the concept, need, planning, importance and philosophy of Work Education and Work Experience.
2. Use chalk-board effectively.
3. Develop an understanding about the potentialities and possibilities inherent in various materials to be used.
4. Develop skills necessary for using such materials and innovative methods to use them.
5. Teach Work Experience with other curricular subjects, develop respect for manual work and a role model in carrying out this work.
6. Relate Work Experience to other curricular subjects.
7. Develop an aesthetic sense for keeping the surroundings beautiful and clean.
8. Evaluate Work Education and Work Experience in terms of process and products.

Chalk Board Writing: **M.M. 30**

Theory

1. Different kinds of chalk boards.
2. Strengths and limitations of chalk writing.
3. Correct use of chalk board writing.
4. Pitfalls in chalk board writing.
5. Use of stencils and multiple chalk-holders on the chalk board.
6. Knowledge of paint and chalk.

Sessional & Practical Work:

1. Writing of English and Hindi letters and numbers in block capital forms and in running hand.
2. Use of coloured chalk.
3. Stick drawing: Human figures, birds and animals.
4. Use of matchstick for drawing.
5. Simple drawing of common subjects such as live flowers, fruits and vegetables.

Preparing Teaching Aids: **M.M.35**

Theory

1. Meaning, Concept and Significance of Teaching Aids.
2. Importance and need of teaching aids.
3. Classifications of teaching aids.
4. Materials required for preparing teaching aid for, e.g. paper, colour, scale, pencil, rubber, etc.
5. Effective use of teaching aids.

Sessional & Practical Work

The student will prepare the following teaching aids:

1. One Raxin Chalk boards, 21/2x31/2, pointer, duster.
2. Ten coloured charts (Full size paper = 20"x30") i.e. five in each teaching subject.
3. One working model, three-dimensional or relief models related to the students teaching subjects.
4. Two slides related to their teaching subject.

Handling of Available Equipment **M.M.35**

Each Teacher Education Institution will make available the following equipments for use of the students.

1. Over head projector
2. Slide projector
3. Tape Recorder
4. Epidiascope
5. TV & Video-cassette-recorder

The students will be required to get acquainted with the major components of the above equipments and their functions. They will be required to use any one of the above equipment, (available in the institution in proper order). They will also prepare a scrap-book and get the same properly checked by concerned teachers.

Annexure VI

Delhi State ETE Syllabus of 'Work Experience' Paper

Unit 1 Concept of Work Exerience

Unit 2 Aims and Objectives

Unit 3 Areas of Work Experience

Unit 4 Planning & organization of Work Experience

Practical Work

II Year

Unit 1 Methodology of teaching Work Experience

Unit 2 Learn Planning in Work Experience

Unit 3 Evaluation in Work Experience

Unit 4 Importance of community in Work Experience in Upper Primary Level

Practical Work

Annexure VII

Some Question Papers on Work Experience

Delhi State ETT 1995
Question Paper
Work Experience

Second Year

Time: 1 ½ Hours [Maximum Marks: 30]

General Instructions:

(i) All questions are compulsory.
(ii) Question numbers 1 to 4 are short-answer type questions of 5 marks each.
(iii) Question number 5 is long-answer type question of 10 marks.

1. You want to organise 'Diwali Mela' in your school. What steps will you take to involve community participation for the success of this Mela?
2. List any four techniques of evaluation of Work Experience activities. Explain one technique and justify its use?
3. "At primary level, for successful implementation of Work Experience Programme, all teachers in schools should work as Work Experience teachers." Discuss.
4. Prepare a lesson-plan for "Cleaning of brass articles" for class IV students. The duration of class is 40 minutes.
5. What do you understand by "Integrated approach"? How can you utilize this approach in Work Experience? Explain with the help of an example.

   OR

   What is meant by "Problem Solving" in Work Experience? Describe the steps involved in a problem solving process?

Delhi State ETT Question Paper Work Experience 1996

Second Year

Time: 1 ½ Hours [Maximum Marks: 20]

General Instructions:

1. All questions are compulsory.
2. All questions carry equal marks.

1. Briefly discuss the importance of work from the point of view of (a) individual development and (b) social development?
2. "Work experience activities are essentially educative activities". Keeping this in view, what criteria will you suggest for selection of Work Experience activities for Delhi schools?
3. What are the objectives of Work-Experience at the Upper Primary stage? How do they differ from those of Primary stage?

   OR

   Give five examples of Work Experience activities each to be undertaken (a) within the school, (b) outside the school for primary school children.
4. Present a lesson plan for the conduct of any service-based activity in your school, indicating clearly the steps in the lesson plan.

Kurukshetra University
B.Ed. Syllabus
Work Experience

M.M. 50

Unit 1 To develop practical skills in the chosen area of Work Experience.

Unit 2 To inculcate a sense of dignity of labour.

Note – Every student shall have to offer one activity out of the following and will be required to keep a record of the work done during the session. Suggested areas of Work Experience are given below:

1. Vegetable growing.
2. Growing of Flowers.
3. Making jellies and pickles.
4. Adult Literacy.
5. Domestic electrical wiring and repairing of house hold appliances such as stove, electric iron, heater, fan, electric tubes, putting a plug on an appliance, mending a fuse, etc.
6. Preparation of items of Interior decoration.
7. Preparation of any four of the following for daily use: Chalk making, Candle making, Ink making, Soap making, Polish making, Liquid Soap, etc.
8. Leather work
9. Book binding
10. Embroidery
11. Knitting
12. Cooking
13. Preparing teaching aids
14. Cutting and tailoring – preparation of any three items
15. Drawing and painting
16. Clay modeling
17. Paper machie
18. Spinning and weaving
19. Cloth weaving and handloom.

Appendix VIII

Sources of A.V. Material and W.E. Equipments

Dealers/Distributors/Producers of Maps and Charts

1. M/s. N.C. Kansil & Sons, Kansil Bhawan, Model Basti, New Delhi-110005
2. M/s. Orient Longman's Ltd., 3/5, Asaf Ali Road, New Delhi-110002.
3. M/s. Prem Educational Stores, 6-B, Prahlad Market, Karol Bagh, New Delhi-110005.
4. M/s. Rajdhani Map Mounting Works, 109/13-A, Chand Mohalla, Gandhi Nagar, Delhi-110032.
5. M/s. Shakun Prakashan, 3625, Netaji Subhash Marg, Darya Ganj, New Delhi-110002.
6. M/s. Universal Map Co., 11-C-92/93, Lajpat Nagar, New Delhi-110024.
7. M/s. United Map Co., A-10/10, Rana Partap Bagh, New Delhi.
8. M/s. Vijay & Co., 8699, Model Basti, New Delhi-110005.
9. M/s. Vidya Chitra Prakashan, 1, Ansari Road, Darya Ganj, New Delhi-110002.
10. M/s. Vigyan Modellers, XN/10685-86, Nanakpura, New Delhi-110005.
11. M/s. Ajanta Publishing House, 9711, Nawab Ganj, Delhi-110006.
12. M/s. Anand Educational Stores, 10-A/37, Shakti Nagar, Delhi-110007.
13. M/s. Audio-Visual Educational Institute, B-339, Mananagar Lucknow.
14. M/s. Bharat Educational Stores, Chhipi Tank, Meerut City.
15. Clifton and Co. (P) Ltd., 12-B, D.B. Gupta Road. Prahlad Markets, New Delhi-110005.
16. M/s. Educational Stores, H-44, Navin Shahdara, Delhi-

1100032.

17. M/s. Gupta Audio-Visual Co., C-23, Subhadra Colony, Sarai Rohilla Delhi-110005.
18. M/s. International Publications, Sadar Thana Road, Delhi-110006.
19. M/s. Indian Book Depot, 2937, Bahadur Garh Road, Delhi-110006.
20. M/s. India Publishing House, B-30, Prahlad Mkt. Karol Bagh, New Delhi-110005.
21. M/s. Capital Map Company, 11-A, Prahlad Mkt., Karol Bagh, New Delhi-110005.
22. Arya Book Depot, 30, Naiwala, Karol Bagh, New Delhi.
23. M/s. India Map Company, 221/41, Padam Nagar, Krishan Ganj, Delhi-110007.
24. M/s. Malhotra Book Stationery Stores, 20/21, Shakti Nagar, Delhi-110007.
25. M/s. Modren Publishing, 2C/39, New Rohtak Road, New Delhi-110005.

Art and Drawing Materials, Display Boards, and other Graphic Materials:

1. M/s. All India Educational Supply Co., Sri. Ram Building Jawahar Nagar, Delhi-110007.
2. M/s. Art Centre, C-56, Gwynne Road, Lucknow-1.
3. M/s. Audio-Visual Educational Institute, B-399, Sector-B, Mahanagar, Lucknow-6 (U.P.)
4. Hrrison Enterprises, C-7/195, Safdarjang Development Area, Hauz Khas, New Delhi-110016.
5. M/s. Clifton & Co. Pvt., 53/2, D.B. Gupta Road, Karol Bagh, New Dlhi-110005.
6. Arya Book Depot., 30, Naiwala, Karol Bagh, New Delhi-110005.
7. M/s. Occaney (India), Factory: B-3/18, Model Town, Delhi-110009, Office : B-5/6, Model Town, Delhi-110009.
8. M/s. Photo Goods Service, 6465, Matra Baryan, Delhi-110006.
9. M/s. Sardana's Art Centre, H.O. WZ/8, Hind Nagar, P.O. Tilak Nagar, New Delhi-110018.

Dealers/Distributors/Producers of Globes:

1. M/s. All India Educational Supply Co. Shri Ram Building Jawahar Nagar Delhi-110007.
2. Capital Map Company, 11-A, Prahlad Mkt., Karol Bagh, New Delhi-110005.
3. M/s. Clifton & Co. Pvt. Ltd., 53/2, D.B, Gupta Road, Karol Bagh, New Delhi-110016.
4. Harrison Enterprises, C-7/195, Safdarjang Development Area, Hauz Khas, New Delhi-110016.
5. M/s. Malhotra Book & Stationery Stores, 20/21, Shakti Nagar, Delhi-110007.
6. M/s. N.C. Kansil & Sons, Kansil Bhawan, Model Basti, New Delhi-110005.
7. Arya Book Depot, 30, Naiwala, Karol Bagh, New Delhi-110005.
8. M/s. Orient Longman's Ltd., 3/5, Asaf Ali Road, New Delhi-110002.
9. M/s. Prem Educational Stores, 6-B, Prahlad Market, Karol Bagh, New Delhi-110005.
10. Bharat Educational Stores, Meerut.

Models:

1. Capital Map Company, 11-A, Prahlad Mkt. Karol Bagh, New Delhi-110005.
2. Harrison Enterprises, C-7/195, Safdarjang Development Area, Hauz Khas, New Delhi-110016.
3. Jain Scientific Equipments, nain Temple Street, Ambala Cantt.
4. M/s. Kalinga Industrial Co., Jain Market, Saudagar Bazar, Ambala Cantt.
5. M/s. N.C. Kansil & Sons, Kansil Bhawan, Model Basti, New Delhi-110005.
6. Arya Book Depot, 30, Naiwala, Karol Bagh, New Delhi-110005.
7. Survey & General Survey of India, Dehra Dun (U.P.)
8. M/s. Vidya Chitra Prakashan, 1, Ansari Road, Darya Ganj, New Delhi-110002.
9. M/s. Young India Films, United India Life Building, F-Block, Cannaught Place, New Delhi.

Photographic Materials:

1. M/s. Imperial Photo Stores, 10, Chandni Chowk, opposite State Bank of India, Delhi-110006.
2. M/s. Mahatta & Company, 59-M, Block, Connaught Circus, New Delhi.
3. Rangoon Studio, Janpath, New Delhi.
4. M/s. Shimla Studio, 4-Regal Building, New Delhi.

Slides in Different Subject Areas:

1. Committee on Science and Technology in Developing Countries and Tata Mc Graw Hill Publishing Co., 12/4, Asaf Ali Road, 3rd Floor, New Delhi.
2. Harrison Enterprises, C-7/195, Safdarjang Development Area, Hauz Khas, New Delhi-110016.
3. Electrofones Science House, Jagadhari Road, Ambala Cantt-133001.
4. Microwave Products India, D-17, D.D.A. Flats, Pandav Nagar, New Delhi-110008.
5. Photographics (Regd.), 1899, Chandni Chowk (Opp. State Bank of India, 2nd Floor, Delhi-110006.
6. M/s. Young India Films, United India Life Building, F-Block, Connaught Place, New Delhi.

16 mm Film Projectors:

1. M/s. Young India Films, United India Life Building, F-Block, Connaught Place, New Delhi.
2. Electronic Instruments and Machinery Corpn.,3, Durlabh Bhawan, Mirza Smail Road, Jaipur-302001.
3. Kehra Instruments (India) P.O. Box No. 2124, Delhi-110007.
4. Cine Sonic Equipment's, F-78, Bhagat Singh Market, New Delhi-110001.
5. Advance Instrument and Chemicals, Copra P.O. Building, Sihani Gate, Ghaziabad (U.P.)

A Comprehensive Bibliography on Work Experience Education

Abdulla, S., "Co-Curricular Activities in Services", in Farooqi, S.A. & Ahmed, eds, *Co-curricular Activities in Schools.* New Delhi: Institute of Advanced Studies in Education, Jamia Millia Islamia, 1996, pp. 150-163.

Aggarwal, JC, *The Progress of Education in Free India.* New Delhi: Arya Book Depot., 1973 (Chapter 26: Work Experience pp. 360-367)

Ahmed, Ikram, "Education of Co-curricular Activities" in Farooqi & ahmed (eds) *Co-curricular Activities in Schools.* New Delhi: Institute of Advanced Studies in Education, Jamia Millia Islamia, 1996, pp. 39-48.

An Approach to Education in Environmental Studies at the Primary Stage. New Delhi: NCERT, 1980.

Art Education: Teachers Hand Book for Class I & II, New Delhi: NCERT, Sept. 1987, .1992.

Avinashilingam, T.S., *Understanding Basic Education.* New Delhi: Ministry of Education, Govt. of India, 1954.

Aziz, Talat, "Psychological and Sociological of Co-Curricular Activities", in *Co-Curricular Activities in Schools*, eds, Farooqi & Ahmed, 1996, pp. 16-23.

Bhatnagar, Romilla, *Fun with Art and Craft.* New Delhi: NCERT, 1993.

Bhatia, H.R., *Craft in Schools*, Bombay : Asia Publishing House.

Bhatia, S.K., "Co-curricular Activities – Conceptual Frame Work" in *Co-curricular Activities in Schools*, eds. Farooqi & Ahmed, New Delhi. IASE, Jamia, 1996, pp 1-6, 85-92.

Choudhary, S.C., "Work Experience and Vocationalization", *Journal of Indian Education* (Vol. 1 No.-1) NCERT, May

1975, pp 41-46.

Choudhary, S.C., *Introducing SUPW in Teacher Education in India*. New Delhi : NCERT, 1982 (Mlimeographed)

Concept of Work Experience, New Delhi : NCERT, 1970.

Craft in Indian School System, New Delhi : NCERT, 1965

Craft in Basic Education, New Delhi: : NCERT, 1965.

Concept of Work Experience, New Delhi : NCERT, 1968.

Dash, B.N., *Principles of Education and Education in the Emerging Indian Society*. Delhi : Ajanta Prakashan, 1986.

De Francesco, Itals H., *Art Education : Literature, Means, & Ends*. New York : Harper $ Row Publishers, 1958.

Dewey John, *Art As Experience*, New York : G.A. Putnam's Sons, 1934.

Dewey, John, *Education As Experience*.

Read, Herbert, *Education Through Art*, New York : Pantheon Books, 1958.

Difficulties of Teachers of Basic Schools, New Delhi : NIBE Educational Reconstruction, Sevagram, Wardha : Hindustani Talimi Sangh, 1937.

Eleventh National Seminar on Elementary Education : Report on Primary Education. New Delhi : NCERT, April 1972.

Exemplar Instructional Material for Work Experience Series

(i) On Leather Work (Classes VI to VIII)

(ii) On Repair and Maintenance of house hold Electrical Appliances (Class IV-X)

(iii) On Plant Protection (Class IX-X)

Farooqi, S.A. & Ahmed, I., (Eds.), *Co-curricular Activities in Schools* New Delhi: Institute of Advanced Studies in Education, Jamia Millia Islamia, 1996.

Farooqi, S.A., "Significance of Co-curricular Activities: A Practical View, in *Ibid*, pp. 24-29.

Faure, Edgar *et al*, *Learning To be: The World of Education: Today & Tomorrow*. (UNESCO). Delhi: Sterling Publishers, 1973.

Goyal, B.R., *The future of 'Work' in Education*. New Delhi: NCERT (Mimeographed Paper)

Guidelines and Syllabus for Upper Primary Stage (Classes VI-VIII), New Delhi: NCERT, 1998.

Hath Kagaz – Monthly Bulletin of the Kumarappa National Handmade Paper Institute, 52/135, Pratap Nagar, Sanganer, Jaipur.

Learning to Do: Towards a Learning and Working Society.

— Report of the National Review Committee on Higher Education with Special Reference to Vocationalization. New Delhi: Ministry of Education & Social Welfare, Govt. of India, 1978.

Hashmi, M., "Dramatics, Theatre and Role Play" in Farooqi & Ahmed, *Op. Cit.*, pp. 73-84.

Hand book for Basic School Teachers. New Delhi: Govt. of India. 1960.

Khan, R.S., "Co-curricular Activities in Social Services", in Farooqi & Ahmed, *Op, Cit.*, pp. 140-149.

Khullar, P.S., "Games and Sports as Part of Co-curricular Activities" in Farooqi & Ahmed, *Op. Cit.*, pp. 93-100.

Kohil. A.S., "Social Service and Community Development Programms at School Level", in Farooqi & Ahmed, *Op. Cit.*, pp. 113-126.

Lulla, B.P. (Compiler), *Child Care* (An English Translation of Shri Gijubhai's *Child Psychology or Bal Darshan.* Bombay: Bombay Teacher Training College, Colaba.

Minimum Levels of Learning at the Primary Stage (Revised), New Delhi : NCERT.

Mukerjee, S., "Development of Aesthetic Sense through Co-curricular Activities" in Farooqi & Ahmed, *Op. Cit.*, pp. 54-62.

Mahmood Sarwar, "Work Experience: its Role in Educational Process" in Farooqi & Ahmed, *Op. Cit.*, pp. 101-112.

Minimum Levels of Learning at Primary Stage, New Delhi: NCERT,

National Policy on Education – 1986, (with Modification undertaken in 1992), New Delhi: Ministry of HRD, Govt. of India, 1992.

National Curriculum for Elementary and Secondary Education. (Revised Version). New Delhi: NCERT, 1988.

National Curriculum for Primary and Secondary Education : A Frame work, New Delhi : NCERT, 1986.

National Scheme of Inservice Training of School Teachers : Resource Material – Part I (General), New Delhi : NCERT, 1987 (Module I : Low Cost Aids for Effective Teaching; Module 13 : Art Education).

Narayan, Shriman, *New Educational Pattern of 10+2.* New Delhi : NCERT, 1978.

Namibiar, K.K. Vijayan, *Work-Experience and Curricular Subjects : An Integrated Approach.* Ambala Cantt : The Indian Publication, 1981.

Pandey R.S. & Sharma, Uma Rani, *Educational Philosophy of Bertnard Russell.* Ambala Cantt : The Associated Publishers, 1990.

Pregramme of Action 1992. New Delhi : Ministry of HRD, Govt. of India, 1992.

Psychology of the Child and the Curriculum, New Delhi : NCERT, 1983.

Ruhela S.P., "*Co-Curricular Activities : A Historical Respective* in Rarooqi & Ahmed, Op cit, pp 7-15.

Report of the Education Commission (1964-66). New Delhi : Govt. of India, Ministry of Education, 1966.

Readings in Basic Education (Vol. II), New Delhi : NIBE, 1968.

Russell, Bertnard, *On Education,* London : George Allen & Unwin, 1926.

Report of the Seminar on "Art and Craft in Teacher Education in Contemporary India. Delhi : Dhanpur Rai & Sons, 1970.

Ruhela, SP. & Vyas K.C., *Sociological Foundations of Educaiton in Contemporary India, Delhi*: Dhanpur Rai & Sons, 1970.

Ruhela S.P. & Khan, R.S. (Eds.) *Joyful Learning : Its Foundations & Implementation.* New Delhi : Regency Publication, 20/36 G. Old Market, West Patel Nagar, 1997.

Sacheti, A.K., Work Experience, *Encyclopedia of Indian Education,* New Delhi:N.C.E.R.T., 2004, pp 1862 to 1868.

Sharma, N., *Value Creators in Education,* New Delhi : Regency Publishers, 1998.

Siddiqui, M.A., "Planning and Organization of Co-curricular

Activities", in Farooqui & Ahmed, *Op Cit*, pp. 30-32.

Srivastava, R.P., "Co-curricular Activities in Languages", in Farooqi & Ahmed, Op. Cit, pp. 128-139.

Seminar on Primary and Work-oriented Education. New Delhi : NCERT, Nov. 1970.

Socially useful Productive Work : Source Book. Vol. III. New Delhi : NCERT, 1981 (I Ed.), Reprinted 1982.

Staley, Eugene, *Work-oriented General Education.* Bombay : Popular Prakashan, 1973.

Samarakoon, Kusuma, *Vocationalization of Education at Plus two Stage in India* – A Revised Learned Paper for M.Phil. New Delhi : Department of Foundation of Education, Faculty of Education, 1986 (Unpublished)

Socially Useful Productive Work : Summer Book Vol. II. New Delhi : NCERT, 1982

Socially Useful Productive Work : Guidelines for Teachers. New Delhi : Central Board of Secondary Education, 1979.

Socially Useful Productive Work Curriculum (Developing and Implementing the Programme)., New Delhi : NCERT, 1979.

Tytler, Jennifer, "Co-curricular Activities and the School Time Table", in Farooqi & Ahmed, *Op. Cit*, pp. 49-52.

Thompson, Merritt M, *The History of Education.* New York : Barnes & Noble Inc., 1951 (III Ed.)

Teachers Guide : Environmental Studies (Class I), New Delhi : NCERT, Sept., 1987.

The Teacher and Education is Emerging Indian Society. New Delhi : NCERT, 1983 (Chapter on 'SUPW', pp. 317-328).

Upadhyay G.C., *Easy to Make Toys and Games.* New Delhi : NCERT, 1993.

Work Experience As An Integral Part of Primary Education. New Delhi : NCERT, 1970

Wickiser, Relfill, *An Introduction to Art Education*, New York : World Book Co.

Wichiser, Relph L., *Education Through Art.*

Wilson, liris H., *Work-Experience in High Schools.* New York : The Ronald Press Co., Q 53.

Work Experience in School Education : Guidelines. New Delhi : NCERT, July 1987.

Work Experience : Classes I & II : Teachers Hand Book, New Delhi NCERT, 1987.

Work Experience : Class III : Teachers Hand Book, New Delhi : NCERT, 1987.

अध्यापक दर्शिका : परिवेशीय अध्ययन (कक्षा 1 के लिए). नई दिल्ली : एन. सी.ई.आर.टी., जुलाई 1987.

कार्यानुभव : अध्यापक दर्शिका (1 और 2 के लिए). नई दिल्ली : एन.सी. ई.आर.टी., 1987.

कार्य अनुभव : कक्षा 3 के लिए : अध्यापक दर्शिका. नई दिल्ली : एन.सी. ई.आर.टी., 1988.

जैन, *कार्य अनुभव* : मेरठ, लायल बुक डिपो

भावे, विनोबा, *शिक्षण विचार*, काशी : अखिल भारत सर्व-सेवा-संघ प्रकाशन. 1960.

स्कूल शिक्षा में कार्यानुभव : मार्ग निर्देश, नई दिल्ली : एन.सी.ई.आर.टी., 1987.

साही, शशिकला, *घरेलू बागवानी*, नई दिल्ली : डायमण्ड पॉकेट बुक्स, 1998.

फोटोग्राफी-अनुदेशात्मक व प्रायोगिक सामग्री कक्षा 9, नई दिल्ली : एन.सी.ई. आर.टी. 1986.

सामाजिक परिवर्तन के लिए प्राथमिक शिक्षा, नई दिल्ली : एन.सी.ई.आर.टी. 1975.

बुनियादी शिक्षा की संकल्पना, नई दिल्ली : एन.सी.ई.आर.टी., 1956.

शिक्षा एवं ग्रामोद्योग (पत्रिका)। उत्तर-प्रदेश खादी तथा ग्रामोद्योग बोर्ड, 8 तिलक मार्ग लखनऊ।

खजूरिया, के.डी. और राही ए.एल., *सामान्य चेतना* (*General Awareness*) कुरुक्षेख : कुरुक्षेत्र विश्वविद्यालय : प्रोढ़ शिक्षा तथा विस्तार केन्द्र

रुहेला, सत्यपाल, *बुनियादी शिक्षा की सामान्य तथा विशिष्ट शिक्षण विधियाँ.* जयपुर : राजस्थान प्रकाशन, 1957 (प्रथम संस्करण) 1966 (चतुर्थ संस्करण)

रुहेला, सत्यपाल, *बुनियादी पाठशाला प्रबंध और स्वास्थ्य रक्षा*, जयपुर : राजस्थान प्रकाशन, 1960 (प्रथम संस्करण) 1966 (तृतीय संस्करण)

रुहेला, सत्यपाल, *शिक्षा का समाज : मूल संप्रत्यय और सिद्धांत*, लखनऊ : उत्तर प्रदेश हिन्दी ग्रंथ अकादमी, 1972.

श्रीवास्तव, आर.पी., *पाश्चात्य शिक्षा शास्त्री*. फैजाबाद : आनन्द प्रकाशन, 1974 (द्वितीय प्रकाशन)

अन्य उपयोगी प्रकाशन

एडगर डेल	अध्यापन में दृश्य-श्रव्य साधन	चण्डीगढ़
गुप्ता आर.एल.	नवीन ज्यामितिय आलेखन	नई दिल्ली
मंगल एस.के.एवं श्रीमती मंगल	दृश्य-श्रव्य शिक्षा	नई दिल्ली
अग्रवाल आर.ए.	भारतीय चित्रकला का विवेचन	मेरठ
जैन जी.सी.	भारतीय चित्रकला-एक विवेचना	मेरठ
हटवाल ए.पी.	विज्ञापन कला	जयपुर
जयदेव आर्य	कला का अध्यापन	आगरा
Arya K.C.	*Simplified Applied Art*	Delhi
Ahluwalia S.L.	*Audio-Visual Hand Book*	Delhi
	Preparing Graphic Aid	Delhi
Chaudhary K.P.	*Audio Visual Aids in Teaching of Indian History*	Delhi
Summer W.L.	*Visual Methods in Education*	Oxford
Green T.L.	*The Visual Approach to Teaching*	London
Wittich W.A. & Schuller C.F.	*Audio Visual Materials*	New York
Firth Brian	*Mass Media in Class Rook*	London
Cochran L.W.	*Manual of Audio-Visual Techniques*	New Delhi
Pula,	*Application & Operation of Audio*	New York
Fred Johad	*Visual Equipment's in Education*	1968
Roberts A.B. & Meknown, H.C.	*Audio Visual Aids to Instruction*	New York

Some important publications on Work Experience published by the NCERT (These ought to be ordered by every college of Education for its library with the Head, Publication Unit, N.C.E.R.T., New Delhi-110016)

1. *Work Experience*
2. *Work Experience* Class III: Teachers Hard Work

3. *Exemplary Instructional Material* for Work Experience as
   - Introduction to House Wiring (Class IX-X)
   - Milk and Milk Products (Class IX-X)
   - General Horticular (Class IX-X)
   - Bee keeping: Insturction-cum-Practical Manual (Class IX-X)
   - Milk Production and Handering (Class IX-X)
   - Plant Protection (Class IX-X)
4. *Poultry Farming* (Text book for Class XI)
5. *Vegetable Production* (Practical Manual for Class XI)
6. *Fundamentals of Horticulture* (Practical Manual for Class XI)
7. *Milk Processes* (Practical Manual for Class XI)
8. *Milk Processing* (Text book for Class XI)
9. *Dairy Technology: Dairy Products* II (Practical Manual for Class XII)

Excellent Books On Personality Development

FOR A BETTER TOMORROW

By: Joginder Singh (Former CBI Director)

This magnum opus by Sh. Joginder Singh is a treatise on self improvement. This win-win sotry is based on the secrets of success as to how to become an achiever. And the success mantra that he espouses for you: Make the best of all opportunities; dream big and work hard—dreams will turn sheer realities. You only need to hone your skills and attitude to become a winner.

Price: Rs. 150/-

WHY WOMEN ARE WHAT THEY ARE

By: Swati Lodha

A book which empowers women to command a unique status, dignity and respect for herself. If you are a daughter, wife or a mother this book will hold your hand and guide you. If you are a son, husband or a father, this book will motivate towards perfection in these roles.

Price: Rs. 195/-

COME ON! GET SET GO...

By: Swati-Shailesh Lodha

This book reveals your real self. It tells you about the hairline difference between a person who is a real success and the one who pretends to be so. This book prompts you to discover yourself. This book doesn't make you "The Best" but it makes you "Second to None".

Price: Rs. 195/-

THE EXCELLENCE IN YOU

By: Dr. Giriraj Shah

This book teaches you to do the same manage your life as a whole. It tells you about your aims in life, how sincerity and perseverance help you to achieve those aims. It teaches you how your presence of mind can make you perfect. It also tells you about various etiquettes, and mannerisms to be used in life.

Price: Rs. 150/-

THE SECRET OF HAPPINESS

By: Jas Mand

This book does not endorse any religious methodology to achieved a state of bliss as most religions claim. The author has attempted to approach the subject of happiness from the scientific angle of a rationalist. Unlike self-help books, it does not offer first-aid. It proposes regular and non-stop work on your growth all the time. The basic emphasis is on cultivating the attitude of happiness, which primarily is in one's own hands.

Price: Rs. 195/-

Fusion Books

X-30, Okhla Industrial Area, Phase-II, New Delhi-110020, Ph.: 41611861, Fax: 41611861,
E-mail: sales@diamondpublication.com, Website: www.diamondpublication.com